ACKNOWLEDGMENTS

This book is dedicated in loving memory of my mother, Claire Feit Swartz, and my grandmother, Beatrice Semel Feit, my first knitting teachers. ■ Special thanks go out to many people who helped make this book possible. To Marilyn Murphy, my good friend and editor—this project has been a great collaboration, just like old times at the Weaving Workshop in Chicago. And to Jean Lampe for your meticulous technical editing. My gratitude goes out to both of you for all your patience, understanding, and support as I knitted through life's challenges. Thanks to Betsy Armstrong, Linda Ligon, Linda Stark, and the entire support staff of Interweave Press who worked so professionally to make the vision of this book a reality. Thanks to Amy Detjen and Lynn Gates for your swift and careful knitting. Thanks to Don Greenwood for the back cover photo. ■ I would like to acknowledge all the yarn companies who so graciously provided yarns used in this book. It is always a pleasure to work with quality materials. ■ Many personal thanks are necessary. First, to my husband, Joel Marcus, for his unfailing love and support and for allowing me the time and space needed to complete this project. To my father, Alex Swartz, and to my late mother, Claire Swartz, for their support, encouragement, and delight in my success. Thanks to my nonknitting sister, Susan Fish, who always appreciates a handknitted gift—maybe this book will finally inspire her to pick up the needles. A special thanks goes out to all the wonderful friends who participated in our Friday Knit Nights in Chicago. We shared a lot of good food, wine, and knitting. May this book inspire new knitters to find the pleasure in knitting and the joy in sharing it that we have found.

TABLE OF CONTENTS

cozy sweater coat on page 84

Tote to school page 12

TECHNIQUES AND TIPS

Mismatched socks . . . page 32

WITHDRAWN

A variety of colors!

Fat hats on page 24

INTRODUCTION

I was lucky enough to learn to knit from my mother and grandmother. I remember the excitement of finally being old enough at age eight to be taught the skill that, for as long as I could remember, I had watched with fascination. I still incorporate some of my mother's and grandmother's idiosyncracies into the way I knit—my method of purling and the way I wind a little ball of extra cast-on yarn. I even have some of their knitting accessories that have now reached vintage status. I love the romantic idea of a craft passed down through the generations much like an oral—or perhaps tactile—history. Whenever I'm knitting, my mother and grandmother are with me. ■ A wonderful phenomenon has been taking place of late. A whole new generation of young adults is falling in love with knitting. Changes in time and philosophy may have diminished the role of family in knitting. Now, in many cases, instead of a vertical passage of knowledge from generation to generation, knowledge is passing laterally within one generation as friend teaches friend. People are finding both a sense of personal satisfaction and community in knitting as avid groups form for the express purpose of being together to knit. It is a time like no other; where it is "hip to knit." ■ In writing this book, I have chosen patterns, styles, yarns, and techniques for today's knitter. My many years of teaching knitting classes and selling yarn have helped me design patterns for the projects that both customers and students want to knit. The projects are presented in a straightforward format, they address frequently asked questions, and they include extra explanations where knitters most often get confused. The projects start with the very simplest and become more sophisticated as you acquire knowledge and skill. The chapter on basics explains everything you need to get started, and it shows the techniques you need to do each of the projects. It's my desire that the experience for all new knitters be positive so that they will find the same pleasure and satisfaction in knitting that I do.

HOW HIP
IS YOUR FIT?

One advantage of knitting your own sweater is your ability to make it exactly the size and fit that you want. With some careful measuring and simple math, alterations to a pattern can be knitted as you go along or, better yet, planned for before you even start. Still, many new knitters are put off by taking measurements and choosing sizes, and they find it a daunting and mystifying task instead of an empowering opportunity.

The first step is to determine which size of pattern instructions to follow. Simply measure an existing garment that fits the way you want your sweater to fit. Lay the garment out on a flat surface and measure the key points—width, length, and sleeve length. Patterns generally include schematic drawings with all key measurements spelled out. Compare these measurements to your garment and choose a corresponding size. Keep in mind, however, that differences in yarn weight and gauge can affect fit. For instance, a sweater knitted with lightweight yarn usually has more ability to drape than a bulky one where extra fabric bunches up.

Next, take into consideration how the garment is to be worn. Do you want it to fit next to your body or over layers of clothes? Is it an outdoor garment for winter or a summer top? A sweater coat, even if it is slim-fitting, requires more ease than a tank top. Note down any changes you make to a pattern, such as "make sleeves two inches shorter." Generally speaking, length measurement changes are easier to adjust than width changes. Therefore, choose the pattern size option closest to the desired width and work from there to personalize the fit.

2

Garments are often described as close-fitting, standard-fitting, loose-fitting or over-sized. These terms refer to the size of the garment in comparison to body measurements, particularly bust/chest circumference. For this reason, you need to measure the bust or chest at the fullest part. A close-fitting garment is the same measurement, or sometimes an inch or two smaller (knits stretch to fit the form.) A standard-fitting garment is about two or three inches larger than the body measurement, or it contains two to three inches of ease. A loose-fitting garment contains about five inches of ease, and an oversized garment is at least six inches larger than the body. Remember that choosing a size by following these guidelines produces a garment sized as the pattern designer intended. However, there is no law that says a knitter must follow these guidelines, and this is where you have the opportunity to individualize the look and fit of a pattern. Just make sure that the lines of the garment lend themselves to your alternative interpretation. For instance: Dropped shoulders generally look better in a garment that is at least somewhat oversized, while set-in and raglan sleeves are pretty versatile and can withstand dramatic changes in fit interpretation. Very full sleeves need to be tapered to keep proportion with a fitted body. If you feel that everything needs changing, you should choose a different pattern.

Fashions change often, but a good sweater design can be timeless. A dated photograph does not necessarily mean a dated design. Too often people cannot see beyond an existing presentation, even as far as changing the color! Sometimes a classic pattern just needs a change in fit to renew it. Would that cardigan be perfect if it were several inches shorter? What if it was body-skimming instead of standard-fitting?

A basic garment can easily go from stodgy to hip with minor alterations. Learning to look critically at a design in order to personalize it is a skill worth developing. *Hip to Knit* includes garments in multiple sizes to accommodate both different shapes and preferences in fit. In choosing patterns to knit, look at basic shapes and then think about how to change them to express the wearer's personality.

FLUFFY
MUFFLER

Extra long, narrow, and lightweight, this mohair scarf can create a dramatic entrance for you. Garter stitch makes it easy to knit. Stripe it by using as few or as many colors as you dare. Try different fringes with each one you make.

■ SIZE

8" (20.5 cm) wide × 80" (203 cm) long (excluding fringe).

■ YARN

Light bulky-weight yarn, about 600 yd (550 m) total.
We used Classic Elite La Gran Mohair (76.5% mohair, 17.5% wool, 6% nylon; 90 yd [82 m]/50g): 1 ball each #6554 French lilac (A), #6527 red (B), #6585 pumpkin (C), #6572 underappreciated green (D), #6515 evergreen (E), #6535 wilted lettuce (F), #6577 blue (G).

■ NEEDLES

Size 10 (6 mm). Adjust needle size if necessary to obtain the correct gauge.

■ NOTIONS

Crochet hook (size G/6 [4mm] or slightly smaller) for attaching fringe. Cardboard square about 6" (15 cm) square for measuring fringe.

■ GAUGE

12 stitches and 22 rows = 4" (10 cm) in garter stitch on size 10 (6 mm) needles.

■ STITCH GUIDE

Garter Stitch
Knit all rows.

■ STRIPE SEQUENCE

4 rows A	2 rows C	2 rows E
2 rows B	6 rows D	4 rows F
2 rows A	2 rows E	6 rows G
6 rows B	2 rows D	2 rows A
4 rows C	2 rows E	2 rows G
2 rows D	2 rows F	

■ SCARF

Loosely cast on 24 stitches. Working in garter stitch, repeat 52-row pattern sequence to a total length of 80" (203 cm). Bind off all stitches loosely.

■ FINISHING

Weave ends in invisibly on back of scarf (see page 6). For fringe, cut twenty-four 12" (30.5 cm) lengths of each color, using cardboard as a guide (see page 7). Attach fringe in six-strand clusters with crochet hook at both ends as follows—starting at left-hand edge: 6 A, 3 A and 3 B, 6 B, 3 B and 3 C, 6 C, 3 C and 3 D, 6 D, 3 D and 3 E, 6 E, 3 E and 3 F, 6 F, 3 F and 3 G, 6 G. Trim fringe ends to even up if necessary.

Use more colors

Try different textures

STRIPES

STRIPES are an easy way to add multiple colors to your work. They can be as narrow or as bold as you desire, and you can use many stripes in one project. Several shades of one hue give a subtle, almost dimensional effect, while contrasting colors make a work vibrate. Stripes are a fun way to experiment with color effects that can be further enhanced by stripe width and placement.

When you're working stripes back and forth in rows, it is easier, but not essential, to work in two-row increments so that all stripes begin on a knit row; in this way the yarn will always be at the edge where you need it. When you're working narrow stripes of just a few colors, it is not necessary to cut the yarn when you change colors—the unused color can be carried loosely up the side of your work for a few rows (Figure 1) or you can carry the colors for more than two rows by twisting the colors every other row (Figure 2). If you are working circularly, the yarn will always be at the beginning of the round.

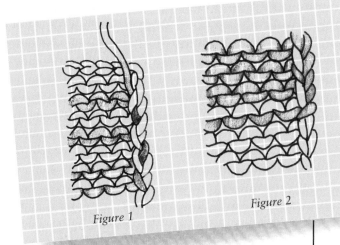

Figure 1

Figure 2

To change colors, simply begin a new row (or round) with your new color. If the edge stitch seems too loose, you can tie the yarn end temporarily (you will undo the knot and work the end in later) to the color you are stopping close to the edge of your work (Figure 3). Proceed with the new color for the desired number of rows and then either return to the original color or add yet another color. When you are finished, work the yarn ends carefully into the backside of the matching color (Figure 4).

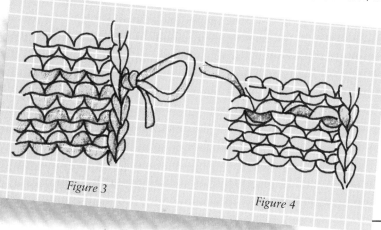

Figure 3

Figure 4

BASIC FRINGE

To cut even lengths of fringe, you will need a piece of stiff cardboard about 1" (2.5 cm) longer than the finished length of the fringe. Starting and ending at the bottom edge, wrap the yarn around the cardboard once for each strand desired. Cut across bottom edge (Figure 1). Bring crochet hook through edge of knitting from front to back (Figure 2). Fold several fringe strands in half and pull fold through work by pulling crochet hook back up so that fringe is about halfway to right side of work (Figure 3). Pull ends of fringe through fold (Figure 4) and pull ends down to straighten and tighten (Figure 5).

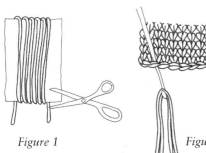

Figure 1

Figure 2

Figure 3

Figure 4

Figure 5

FANCIER FRINGE

Double Knotted Fringe

Begin with basic fringe. Work a second row of knots below the basic row by taking half the fringe strands from the first and second group and knotting them together in a square knot between the two (Figure 1). Repeat knotting process across fringe about 1" (2.5 cm) below previous knots, using alternate fringe strands (Figure 2).

Figure 1

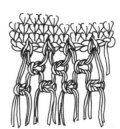

Figure 2

TWISTED FRINGE

Begin with basic fringe with just a few strands per group. Secure work to table by weighting it down to keep it in place. Take two adjacent groups, one in each hand, and twist them both in the same direction as tightly as possible (Figure 1). Put both groups in one hand and let them twist back on themselves (Figure 2). Knot close to bottom (Figure 3).

Figure 1

Figure 2

Figure 3

This is a mohair blend

SCARF

A simple texture stitch can dramatically enhance the effect of a multicolored yarn. Subtle color changes are spun into this yarn to create painterly stripes; all you have to do is knit merrily along—the color changes just happen! Seed stitch keeps the scarf from curling at the edges and creates a reversible fabric. Individualize the look with your choice of fringe or edge finish.

■ SIZE	■ YARN	■ NEEDLES	■ NOTIONS	■ GAUGE
About 9" (23 cm) wide × 60" (152.5 cm) long.	Worsted-weight yarn, about 420 yd (385 m). We used Eisaku Noro Kureyon (100% wool; 110 yd [100 m]/50 g): 4 balls #52 green blue.	Size 9 (5.5 mm). Adjust needle size if necessary to obtain the correct gauge.	Tapestry needle.	16 stitches and 28 rows = 4" (10 cm) in seed stitch on size 9 (5.5 mm) needles.

■ STITCH GUIDE

Seed Stitch (worked over an odd number of stitches)

Row 1: *Knit 1, purl 1*; repeat from * to * across row, end knit 1.

Repeat this row throughout for pattern.

■ SCARF

Loosely cast on 35 stitches. Work in seed stitch to a total length of 60" (152.5 cm). Bind off all stitches loosely. Using a tapestry needle, weave in loose ends at beginning and end of scarf.

Seed

DESIGNING YOUR OWN SCARF

A scarf is one of the easiest pieces to design, and these tips will ensure a professional looking result. First, figure out the size you want the scarf to be. Then you'll need to figure out how many stitches to cast on. Multiply your knitting gauge (see Basics, page 90) by the desired width of the finished scarf. For example, if your gauge is 4 stitches to the inch and the scarf is to be 9" (23 cm) wide (average width is 8–12" [20.5–30.5 cm]), you will cast on 36 stitches. The average length of a scarf is 48–60" (122–152.5 cm).

But what about choosing a stitch pattern? Stockinette stitch (knit on right side, purl on wrong side) causes the lengthwise edges of your scarf to curl under and the short ends to curl up. If you want flat edges, you need to balance the number of knit and purl stitches on each side of your scarf either throughout or at least at the edges. Stitches like seed or moss stitch, basketweave stitches or rib stitches are ideal for scarves because they are both balanced and reversible. Garter stitch works too because it's all knit with no purl stitches. Remember that you may have to adjust your stitch count from the gauge measurement count to accommodate the number of stitches for your pattern repeat (see Basics, page 89).

Another point of consideration is how you cast on and bind off. If you tend to cast on or bind off tightly, it is a good idea to use a needle one or two sizes larger. A larger needle will prevent the horizontal edges from pulling in.

Make your gauge swatch in the stitch you are planning to knit the scarf in and remember that it is generally desirable that a scarf fabric have more drape than a sweater. Therefore, a scarf is usually worked with needles one or two sizes larger than one would choose for a sweater of the same yarn.

The amount of yarn required will vary with the width and length of the scarf, but you can estimate using about 30% of the yarn needed for an average sweater. In sport-weight yarn estimate using about 480 yd (439 m), in worsted-weight yarn 420 yd (384 m), and bulky yarn 300 yd (275 m). However, some stitch patterns use more yarn than others. To make sure you have sufficient amounts of yarn, check the number of square inches completed with the first full skein in the chosen stitch pattern and gauge. Then divide that number of square inches into the total square inches in your scarf. For example, if one skein makes 9" in width by 20" in length (23 x 51 cm), that equals 180 square inches. If your finished scarf is to be 9" by 60" (23 x 152.5 cm), it will have 540 square inches, not including fringe. Divide the 180 square inches made by the first skein into the 540 square inches needed to complete the scarf, and the result is 3. You will therefore need at least 3 skeins to complete the scarf, plus extra yarn for the fringe.

Basketweave

Rib

Make it bigger or smaller. How about using different buttons?

FELTED
TOTE BAG

This is magic indeed—knit the tote, wash it, and it shrinks and bulks up. The process of felting not only gives this color-block tote bag a unique finish, it adds to the stability of the fabric.

SIZE

After Felting: Strap and side piece about 3" × 72" (7.5 × 183 cm); Front and back pieces about 14" × 15" (35.5 × 38 cm); Pocket about 7½" × 9" (19 × 23 cm). Before Felting: Strap and sides about 3¾" × 84" (9.5 × 213 cm); Front and back pieces about 16" × 20" (40.5 × 51 cm); Pocket about 7¾" × 10" (19.5 × 25.5 cm).

YARN

Worsted-weight yarn, about 250 yd (229 m) of colors A and B, 200 yards (183 m) color C, 100 yards (91 m) color D.
We used Baabajoes Wool Pak Yarns NZ 10 ply (100% wool; 430 yards [393 m]/250 g): 1 skein each Red (A), Sunshine (B), Gold-stone (C), and Softsun (D).

NEEDLES

Size 8 (5 mm). Adjust needle size if necessary to obtain proper gauge.

NOTIONS

Crochet hook size D/3 (3.25 mm).

GAUGE

17 stitches and 24 rows = 4" (10 cm) in stockinette stitch on size 8 (5 mm) needles before felting; 19 stitches and 28 rows = 4" (10 cm) after felting.

Note: Felting is not an exact science. As you'll see on page 15, many variables can affect the degree of felting and shrinkage.

BLANKET STITCH is one of the simplest and most versatile embroidery stitches. It can be used to decorate an edge or, if the stitches are placed close together, it becomes a buttonhole stitch which also covers, protects, and stabilizes an edge. It is easy to work the blanket stitch evenly on knitting because one can use the knitted stitch as a spacing guide. Thread a length of yarn about 24" (61 cm) through a tapestry needle. Anchor yarn at edge and bring needle through fabric from front to back, about ¼" (6 mm) below edge. Pull needle toward top edge with yarn end in back of needle (Figure 1). Working from left to right, repeat process across top of work, spacing stitches evenly about ¼" (6 mm) apart (Figure 2). Fasten off.

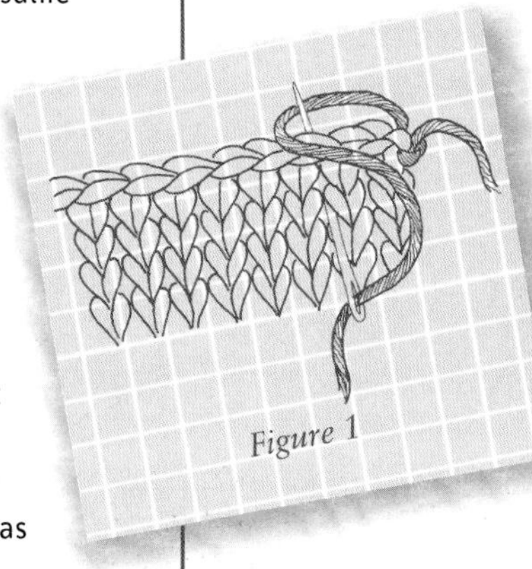

Figure 1

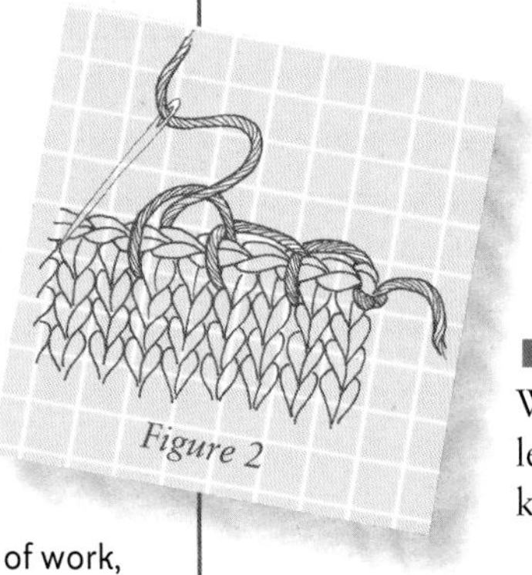

Figure 2

STITCH GUIDE

Garter Stitch
Knit all rows.

FRONT

With color A, cast on 68 stitches. Work 1" (2.5 cm) in garter stitch. On next row (wrong side of work) knit 6, purl 56, knit 6. Knit next row. Repeat these 2 rows until piece measures 19" (48.5 cm) from cast-on edge. Work 1" (2.5 cm) in garter stitch. Bind off all stitches.

BACK

Work same as front, using color B.

POCKET

With color B, cast on 32 stitches. Work 1" (2.5 cm) in garter stitch. On next row (wrong side of work) knit 4, purl 24, knit 4. Knit next row. Repeat these 2 rows until piece measures 9" (23 cm) from cast-on edge. Work 1" (2.5 cm) in garter stitch. Bind off all stitches.

STRAP AND SIDES

With color C, cast on 14 stitches. Work in garter stitch for a total length of 84" (213 cm), slipping first stitch of each row as if to knit (see Basics, page 92). Bind off all stitches.

Weave in all loose ends. Slipstitch (see Basics, page 93) cast-on edge of strap and sides to bound-off edge. Placing this seam at the bottom corner of front, use safety pins to pin front to strap and sides, butting edges and easing strap around corners. Slipstitch strap and side to front. Repeat for back, making sure that top edges and bottom corners of back are even with front. Felt bag and pocket separately. Slipstitch pocket to front, centering pocket sides on front and placing pocket about 2½" (6.5 cm) from top edge. Using contrasting colors, work blanket stitch (see page 14) evenly around top edges of front, back and pocket. For top closure, cut one strand each of color A, B and C about 30" (76 cm) long. Using a crochet hook, pull through center top of back about ½" (1.3 cm) below center top. Hold ends even (you now have 6 ends) and work a tight three-strand braid of two ends each for a total length of 8" (20.5 cm). Knot ends and trim to ½" (1.3 cm). Repeat process for pocket closure, using three 24" (61 cm) lengths of color C and using crochet hook to pull through front above pocket 1" (2.5 cm) from either edge. Braid to a total length of 6" (15 cm). Knot and trim ends. Sew larger button at center front 1" (2.5 cm) below top edge with matching yarn color (see Sewing on a Button, page 61). Sew smaller buttons to pocket top about 1" (2.5 cm) from top and side edges creating shank as for top. To close bag or pocket, wrap braid around shank.

Three-strand braid

FELTING is a process of fulling a wool or animal fiber to create a thicker, denser fabric with a soft finish. Felting causes the item to shrink in size as fibers "lock" together. The wool can be knitted, woven, or even fashioned in unspun or roving form. It is important for the fiber to be wool that has not been treated to be a superwash. Because results can vary widely, it is a good idea to test the felting process with swatches and take careful notes and measurements. Variables such as the yarn itself, different colors of the same yarn, water temperature, and soap can all affect the final product. Felting occurs when the fiber is "shocked" by contrasts in temperature and agitation. Simple felting can be done in the washing machine, using a hot wash and cold rinse in a regular cycle. Use a mild detergent such as soap flakes. Placing the item in an old pillowcase will aid the agitation process (fibers rubbing against each other) as well as keep loose fibers from clogging the washing machine. Put towels in the washing machine to aid in the agitation. The felted item can be dried in the dryer, although this extra step is usually not necessary to the felting process. If the item does not shrink sufficiently during washing, repeat the process until you achieve the desired size. Remember that it is next to impossible to reverse the felting process so it's better to go slowly, reducing the size by increments.

BARE NECESSITIES
PURSE

Knit in metallic and it becomes an evening bag. Knit in cotton and throw it on
with your jeans. Either way it's that little purse that's just enough to hold keys,
lipstick, cell phone, driver's license, and some money—the bare necessities.

■ SIZE	■ YARN	■ NEEDLES	■ NOTIONS	■ GAUGE
About 5½" (14 cm) wide and 7" (18 cm) long plus strap.	Double-knitting (DK) weight yarn, about 150 yd (138 m). We used Berroco Metalica (85% rayon, 15% metallic; 85 yd [78 m] /25g): 2 balls # 1003 black/gold.	Size 7 (4.5 mm); I-cord strap—Size 3 (3 mm): 2 double-pointed needles; cable needle. Adjust needle size if necessary to obtain correct gauge.	Four safety pins or pieces of contrasting yarn for marking edges; three beads with large center holes, and/or three coins with large center hole or choice of trim and closure.	23 stitches and 32 rows = 4" (10 cm) in stockinette stitch on size 7 (4.5 mm) needles.

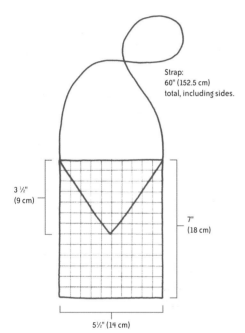

Strap: 60" (152.5 cm) total, including sides.

3 ½" (9 cm)

7" (18 cm)

5½" (14 cm)

■ **STITCH GUIDE**
Stockinette Stitch
Row 1: (right side) Knit all stitches.
Row 2: Purl all stitches.
Repeat Rows 1 and 2 for pattern.

■ **ABBREVIATIONS**
ssk slip, slip, knit (see page 23)
Slip two stitches knitwise, one at a time, onto the right needle. Insert point of left needle into front of two slipped stitches and knit them together through back loops with right needle.
sssk Work as for ssk, using 3 stitches.

■ **BAG**
Cast on 32 stitches. Knit 3 rows. Change to stockinette stitch and work until piece measures 14" (35.5 cm) marking edges at 7"(18 cm) and at 14" (35.5 cm) and ending with a wrong-side row.
Shape flap:
Row 1: Knit 2, ssk, knit to last 4 stitches, knit 2 together, knit 2.
Row 2: Purl.
Repeat these 2 rows 12 more times—6 stitches remain. On next row, knit 1, slip next 2 stitches to cable needle (see page 26) and hold in front of work, knit next 2 stitches, knit 2 stitches from cable needle, knit 1. Purl 1 row.

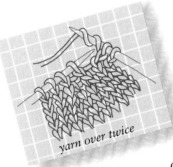

yarn over twice

Make buttonhole loop:
On next row, knit 2, yarn over twice, ssk, knit 2. *Next Row:* Purl to first yarnover and drop loop from needle, purl next yarnover, purl remaining stitches. On next row, sssk, knit 3 together—2 stitches remain. Bind off remaining 2 stitches. Cut yarn, leaving about a 6" (15 cm) tail and thread tail through last stitch and tighten.

Strap: With double-pointed needle, cast on 3 stitches to make I-cord. *Row 1:* Knit. *Row 2:* Do not turn work. Slide work to opposite end of needle, pull yarn around back of work and knit 3 stitches. Repeat Row 2 until strap measures 60" (152.5 cm). Bind off.

■ **FINISHING**

With tapestry needle, weave in all loose ends to wrong side of work and secure. Fold bag, matching markers. Sew side seams using mattress stitch (see Basics, page 92). Place one coin and bead at either end of strap and knot below to hold in place, leaving about a 1" (2.5 cm) end. Sew strap in place using the slipstitch stitching (see Basics, page 93) along side seams. Fold flap down and mark closure placement. Sew bead/coin in place at marker.

I-CORD

According to knitter's mythology, the "I" in I-cord stands for idiot. However, there is nothing idiotic about this clever method of creating a neat and sturdy tubular cord. I-cord can be knitted on its own, or it can be knitted directly into a garment, often as an edging or as a topknot on a hat.

I-cord is worked using two double-pointed needles, usually several sizes smaller than the main body of the garment to assure a firm cord. Cast on the desired number of stitches, usually three to five. *Without turning the needle, slide the stitches to the opposite end of the right-hand needle and switch that needle to the left hand and the empty needle to the right hand. The stitches are now in a "ready-to-knit" position—*except* the yarn is coming from the stitch at the far end of the needle instead of the first stitch. Pull the yarn across the back of the work and use it to knit the stitches. Repeat from *. After a few rows, the work will start becoming tubular. Repeat from * until I-cord is desired length. Bind off.

MOST BASIC
HAT

Don't be caught without this hat. It's basic, head-hugging, and easily adapted to endless possibilities. The hat shown is knitted in stockinette stitch, but you can knit the edges and/or other areas in garter or seed stitch. Or use this solid-colored base as your palette and embroider freely. Work as many colors as you dare into one hat with a rainbow of stripes. Or detail it with only a soft roll at the edge and subtle lines created by shaping the crown, and your hat can become as individual as your head.

great looking decorative decreases

■ SIZE	■ YARN	■ NEEDLES	■ NOTIONS	■ GAUGE
To fit an average adult's head about 21" (54.5 cm) in circumference, finished length (unrolled) about 9½" (24 cm) long.	Worsted-weight yarn about 150 yd (138 m). We used Rowan Kid Classic (70% lambs wool, 26% kid mohair, 4% nylon; 151 yd [138 m]/50 g): 1 ball #835 purple for solid hat, or 1 ball each #835 purple and #827 orange for striped hat.	Size 8 (5 mm). Adjust needle size if necessary to obtain the correct gauge.	Tapestry needle	19 stitches and 26 rows = 4" (10 cm) in stockinette stitch on size 8 (5 mm) needles.

■ **STITCH GUIDE**
Stockinette Stitch
Row 1: (right side) Knit all stitches.
Row 2: Purl all stitches.
Repeat Rows 1 and 2 for pattern.

SOLID HAT

Cast on 99 stitches. Work in stockinette stitch until piece measures 7" (18 cm) unrolled or desired length from beginning, ending with a wrong-side row.
Shape top:
Row 1: (right side) *Knit 7, knit 2 stitches together*. Repeat from * to * across row—88 stitches remain.
Row 2: (and all wrong-side rows) Purl.
Row 3: *Knit 6, knit 2 stitches together*. Repeat from * to * across row—77 stitches remain.
Row 5: *Knit 5, knit 2 stitches together*. Repeat from * to * across row—66 stitches remain.
Continue in this manner, working 1 less stitch between decreases until 22 stitches remain. On next right-side row knit 2 stitches together across row—11 stitches remain. Purl one row. Cut yarn, leaving a tail about 18" (46 cm) long. Using a tapestry needle, thread tail through remaining stitches and pull tight (see page 30). Use remainder of tail to sew center back seam using mattress stitch (see Basics, page 92) and reversing seaming at bottom edge for about 1½" (3.8 cm) to allow for roll. Weave in loose ends.

STRIPED HAT

With orange, cast on as for solid hat. Work even for 4" (10 cm) unrolled or desired length from beginning. Alternate 4 rows purple and 4 rows orange until piece measures 7" (18 cm) from cast-on edge, unrolled. Shape top as for solid hat but alternate colors every 2 rows. Finish as for solid hat.

22

DECORATIVE DECREASES

Decreasing can be a design element in a piece that also provides shaping. By using a specific type of decrease placed at specific points, you can create lines that give the appearance of folds in the top of the hat. In this case, the decrease is a knit 2 together (see Basics, page 92) that causes a slant to the right. By working one less stitch between decreases each time you knit a decrease row, you place decreases so they line up on top of one another and seem to join in a slanting line.

There are several decrease methods that can be used to work left-slanting decreases. Instead of a knit 2 together decrease, you can either slip one stitch to the right- hand needle, knit the next stitch, and then pass the slipped stitch over the knitted stitch (skp-Figures 1 & 2).

Or knit 2 stitches together through the back loop (k tbl-Figure 3). Or slip 2 stitches one at a time knitwise to the right-hand needle and knit them together through the front loops with the tip of the left-hand needle (ssk-Figures 4 & 5). Aligning placement of any of these decrease methods creates lines slanting to the left.

In stitch patterns, such as lace patterns, where decreases are necessary to keep stitch counts constant as new stitches are created in the openwork, you'll often find a combination of both left- and right-slanting decreases used in deliberate placement to articulate motifs within the pattern.

skp
Figure 1

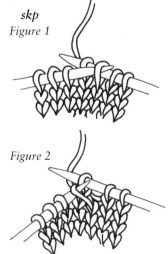

Figure 2

k tbl
Figure 3

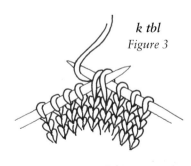

ssk
Figure 4

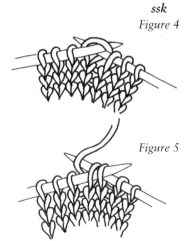

Figure 5

Make hats in different colors for your friends

FAT HATS

These hats add a little fun to a winter wardrobe. Knitted in two variations with super chunky yarns, they're quick to work up and they introduce two simple but striking pattern stitches—cables and seed stitch.

▪ SIZE

To fit an average adult's head about 21" (53.5 cm) circumference.

▪ YARN

Gathered Top: Super chunky-weight yarn, about 120 yd (110 m). We used Tahki Baby (100% merino wool; 60 yd [55 m]/100 g); 2 balls, #8 soft orange.
Two-Tassel Top: Super chunky-weight yarn, about 120 yd (110 m). We used Classic Elite Weekend Waterspun (100% merino wool; 57 yd [52 m]/100 g); 2 skeins, #7235 chartreuse.

▪ NEEDLES

Gathered Top: Size 11 (8 mm) and 13 (9 mm). Two-Tassel Top: Size 10½ (6.5 mm) and 11 (8 mm). Adjust needle size if necessary to obtain the correct gauge.

▪ NOTIONS

Tapestry needle; piece of lightweight cardboard about 4" (10 cm) square for tassel making.

▪ GAUGE

Gathered Top: 9 stitches and 12 rows = 4" (10 cm) in stockinette stitch on size 13 (9 mm) needles. Two-Tassel Top: 9 stitches and 12 rows = 4" (10 cm) in stockinette stitch on size 11 (8 mm) needles.

Attach the tassels to the end of a yarn braid

CABLES are made by changing the order of the stitches on your needle to create a twisted, ropelike appearance. Typically, an even-numbered group of knit stitches is set off by at least one purl stitch on each side (Figure 1). For a temporary stitch holder, use a cable needle, a short double-pointed needle that is shaped either straight, straight with a dip in the middle, or like a U (Figure 2). (The "best" style of cable

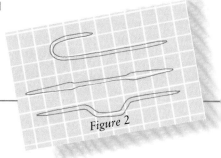

Figure 1

needle to use is strictly a matter of personal preference.) At a determined point in your pattern you will be instructed to slip a certain number of stitches to the cable needle. For the sake of our example, let's say your cable pattern is 6 stitches. You'll slip 3 stitches to the cable needle and

Figure 2

Make the tassels

another color

■ **STITCH GUIDE**

1 × 1 Rib (worked over an even number of stitches)
Row 1: *Knit 1, purl 1*. Repeat from * to * across row.
Row 2: *Work as Row 1.
Repeat Rows 1 and 2 for pattern.

Seed Stitch (worked over an even number of stitches)
Row 1: *Knit 1, purl 1*. Repeat from * to * across row.
Row 2: *Purl 1, knit 1*. Repeat from * to * across row.
Repeat Rows 1 and 2 for pattern.
Note: If you are working with an odd number of stitches Row 2 will be the same as Row 1.

4-Stitch Front-Cross Cable (worked over 6 stitches)
Row 1: (right side of work) Purl 1, slip next 2 stitches to cable needle and hold in front of work. Knit next 2 stitches. Slip 2 stitches from cable needle back to left-hand needle and knit these 2 stitches. Purl 1.
Rows 2, 4 and 6: Knit 1, purl 4, knit 1.
Rows 3 and 5: Purl 1, knit 4, purl 1.
Repeat Rows 1–6 for pattern.

■ **GATHERED TOP**

With smaller needles, cast on 52 stitches. Work 2½" (6.5 cm) in 1 × 1 Rib, ending with wrong-side row. Change to larger needles and set up pattern as follows: (right side) *Purl

To make a **TASSEL**, cut a piece of cardboard 3–5" (7.5–12.5 cm) wide and 1" (2.5 cm) longer than the desired length of your tassel. Beginning and ending at the same bottom edge, securely wrap yarn around cardboard (Figure 1), but not too tight, until you reach the desired fullness of the tassel. (Tip: If you have to make more than one tassel per piece, count the number of wraps so your tassels will be consistent.) Cut a

length of yarn at least 12" (30.5 cm) long and thread through a tapestry needle. Slip needle underneath wrapped yarn at

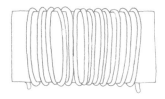

Figure 1

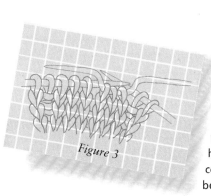

then hold these stitches in front or in back of your work (Figure 3). The front or back placement determines the direction the cable will twist. Knit the next 3 stitches on your needle, then slip the 3 stitches from the cable needle back to the left hand needle and knit those stitches to complete the cable (Figure 4). On rows between cable twists, work stitches as they appear (knit the knits and purl the purls.) Your pattern will indicate the number of rows the cable will be repeated. Fewer rows between twists will create a more pronounced cable.

Figure 3

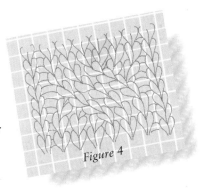

Figure 4

1, knit 3, increase 1 stitch (see Basics, page 91) purl 1, work next 8 stitches in Row 1 of seed stitch *. Repeat from * to * across row—56 stitches. On next row * work 8 stitches in Row 2 of seed stitch, knit 1, purl 4, knit 1*. Repeat from * to * across row. Pattern placement is now established (see Basics, page 90). On next row, begin with Row 1 of both seed stitch and 4-stitch front-cross cable patterns. Work even in patterns as established until work measures 8" (20.5 cm) from beginning, ending with a wrong-side row. *Shape crown:* On next row (right side of work is facing) knit 1, *knit 3 together; repeat from * across row to last stitch, knit 1—20 stitches. Purl 1 row. Knit 2 together across next row—10 stitches. Cut yarn, leaving a tail about 20" (51 cm) long. Thread tail through tapestry needle and thread needle through remaining 10 stitches on knitting needle (see page 30). Pull yarn tail firmly to close up stitches. Use remainder of tail yarn to sew invisible seam on right side of work using mattress stitch (see Basics, page 92). Make tassel wrapping yarn about 30 times and attach to center top of hat.

■ **TWO-TASSEL TOP**

Work same as for Gathered Top (using smaller needles if necessary) until work measures 8½" (21.5 cm). Bind off all stitches. Sew vertical seam from right side of work using the mattress stitch for an invisible seam, creating a tube. Turn hat inside out and stitch horizontal seam across top of hat using backstitch (see Basics, page 92), aligning cables so that they will meet at horizontal seam. Make two tassels as for Gathered Top except wrap tassels about 24 times each. Attach at top corners of hat.

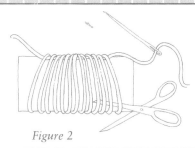

Figure 2

upper edge, pull together tightly, and fasten with a knot. Leave the yarn tail to sew tassel to hat. Cut through yarn at lower edge (Figure 2). Take a second length of yarn and wrap it securely around the tassel several times just below the top-edge knot (Figure 3). Knot securely, thread ends onto tapestry needle and pull to center of tassel. Trim ends even at bottom edge.

Figure 3

TRICOLORED
STOCKING CAP

Try this one on for size—a classic ribbed stocking cap that James Dean would have lusted after. Knitted in merino wool, it is so soft and itch-free, you'll want to wear it all the time. The 2×2 rib stretches to accommodate most heads, and the turned-back cuff provides extra warmth around the ears.

■ SIZE

To fit an average adult's head about 21" (53.5 cm) in circumference, finished length of hat (unfolded) about 11" (28 cm) long.

■ YARN

Double-knitting (DK) weight yarn, about 275 yd (252 m). We used Filatura di Crosa Zara (100% merino wool; 137 yd [125 m]/50 g): 1 ball each #1657 bronze (A), #1469 charcoal (B) and #1490 denim blue (C).

■ NEEDLES

Size 6 (4 mm), set of 4 double-pointed needles and 16" (40-cm) circular needle (optional). Adjust needle size if necessary to obtain the correct gauge.

■ NOTIONS

Tapestry needle; stitch markers.

■ GAUGE

23 stitches and 28 rows = 4" (10 cm) in stockinette stitch on size 6 (4 mm) needles. 28 stitches and 30 rows = 4" (10 cm) in 2 × 2 rib (slightly stretched) on size 6 (4 mm) needles.

■ STITCH GUIDE

2 × 2 Rib (worked over a multiple of 4 stitches)
Row 1: *Knit 2, purl 2*. Repeat from * to * across row (or round).
Row 2: Work stitches as they appear.
Repeat Rows 1 and 2 for pattern.

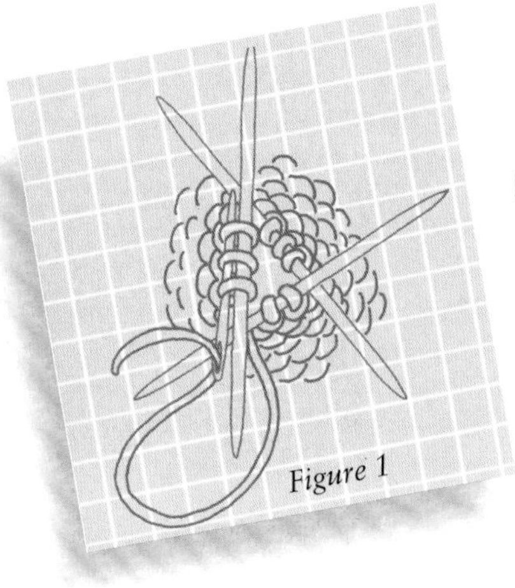

■ STOCKING CAP

With bronze (A) and circular or double-pointed needle, cast on 128 stitches. Join, being careful not to twist stitches (see page 31). Work even in 2 × 2 Rib until piece measures 5" (12.5 cm). Change to charcoal (B) and work another 3" (7.5 cm). Change to denim blue (C), and work ½" (1.3 cm) even, placing a marker after every 8th stitch in last round.

Shape top: If using circular needle, change to double-pointed needles dividing stitches evenly among needles. *Work to 2 stitches before marker, purl 2 together*. Repeat from * to* across round. Work 1 round even, working stitches as they appear (knit the knit stitches, purl the purl stitches). On next round and subsequent alternate rounds, work to 2 stitches before each marker and then decrease by either knitting 2 stitches together or purling 2 stitches together as needed to maintain continuity of rib pattern. When 2 stitches remain between each marker, knit 2 stitches together around—16 stitches remain. Knit next round removing all markers. On next round, knit 2 stitches together around—8 stitches remain.

Cut yarn, leaving a tail about 8" (20.5 cm) long. Using a tapestry needle, thread tail through remaining stitches (Figure 1). Pull tight, secure, and fasten off. Weave in loose ends.

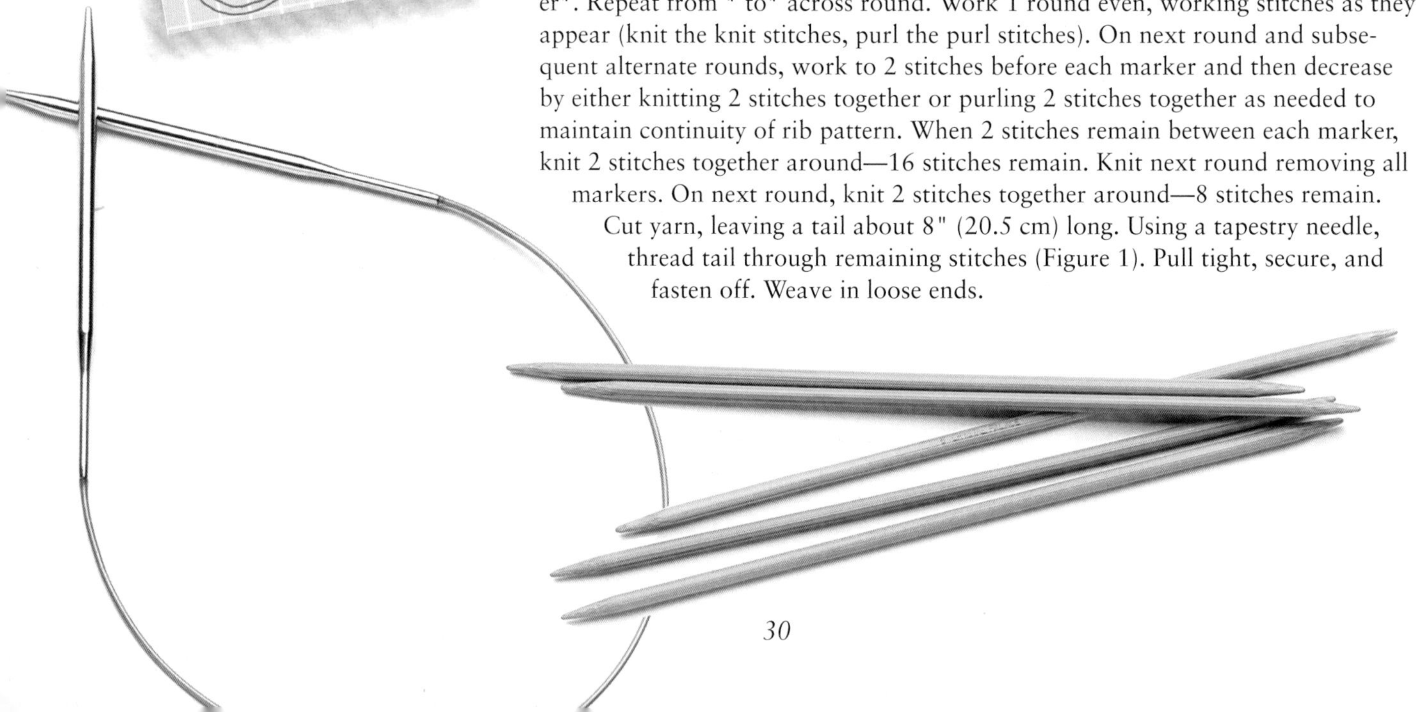

Figure 1

CIRCULAR KNITTING

Being able to knit circular to create a tubular fabric has one big advantage—no seams. However, you will need an array of sizes in double-pointed (sets of four or five) and circular needles. Circular needles are available in different lengths, the most common being 16"(40-cm), 24" (60-cm) and 29" (74-cm). The circular needle used must be shorter than the circumference of the garment. You can compact the stitches on the needle but you can't stretch out work that is too narrow. The shortest circular needle available is 16" (40-cm) so any garment with a narrower circumference, such as socks or gloves, must be worked on double-pointed needles which can accommodate as little as one stitch per needle. A 16" (40-cm) needle is a good length for a hat with a 21" (53.5 cm) circumference but you'll need to switch to double-pointed needles as you begin decreasing to shape the crown.

Pattern directions for circular knitting call the rows "rounds." The major difference between working in rounds and working back and forth in rows is that when you're working in rounds, you don't turn the work. Since the right side of the work is always facing you, you don't need to change knit stitches to purl stitches on the wrong side of the work. For this reason, if you are working in rounds in stockinette stitch, every stitch will be a knit stitch. If you are working in rounds in ribbing, simply work each stitch as it appears to maintain the continuity of the rib.

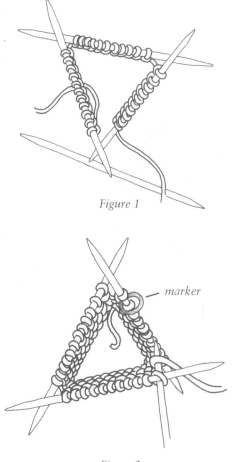

Figure 1

Figure 2

The trickiest part of circular knitting is getting started. Whether you're using circular or double-pointed needles, cast on the required number of stitches all on one needle. If you're using double-pointed needles, after casting the stitches on to one needle, divide the total number of stitches evenly between three or four needles (needles come in sets of four or five, but you need one to knit with) by sliding stitches over from either end. Make sure that the stitches don't twist in this process and that the cast-on edge is at the bottom of the needle. Once you have the stitches on your needles, arrange them in a circle or triangle with the point of the first cast-on stitch in your left hand and the last cast-on stitch in your right hand (Figure 1). Now you're ready to join your work.

With the spare needle, begin to knit with the yarn from the right-hand needle, pulling the first stitch firmly to eliminate a gap. After the first stitch use a marker to mark the beginning of each new round (Figure 2). You'll slip this marker as you work each round. Work to the end of the first needle and use that needle as a spare to work stitches from the next needle. Continue in this manner around.

If you're using circular needles, take the opposite point of the needle (the first stitch you cast on will be here) in your left hand and begin knitting with the point of the needle in your right hand. Place a marker on the needle to designate the beginning of the round as above.

MISMATCHED STRIPED
SOCKS

Satisfaction guaranteed. Socks are small enough to
progress quickly, even on small needles. Their portability
makes them great for car trips or knitting in small spaces.
The magic in turning a heel never ceases to amaze most knitters. The biggest challenge is making two socks come out
exactly the same size. These socks feature stripes not only for
the sake of design but also as a counting device—as long as the
numbers add up, your socks will come out the same size. But
why make identically striped twins when fraternal twins can
be so much more interesting?

The color and striping possibilities are endless

To fit a woman's (man's) medium foot: 9½" (10½") (24 [26.5] cm) from tip of heel to tip of toe. Cuff: 6" (7") (15 [18] cm) long. These measurements are easily adjusted for a custom fit (see page 37).

Double-knitting (DK) weight yarn, about 100 yd (91m) of each color.
Variation I (on pages 32–33): We used Rowan Rowanspun DK (100% wool; 219 yd [200 m]/50 g): 1 skein each # 735 green (A), #734 blue (B), #731 orange (C), #738 pale grey (D). Variation II (on page 35): We used Tahki/Stacy Charles Zara (100% merino wool, 136 yd [125 m]/50 g): 1 skein each #1523 plum (A), #1666 magenta (B), #1667 red orange (C), #6053 dusty lavender (D).

Size 3 (3.25 mm) set of 4 double-pointed needles. Adjust needle size if necessary to obtain the correct gauge.

Tapestry needle; stitch marker.

KITCHENER STITCH

Kitchener stitch is a method of grafting stitches together invisibly, and it closely resembles the knitted stitch. Used to finish off the toe of a sock, it also grafts the stitches with no added bulk at the toe. To graft the toe of a sock, evenly divide toe stitches on two knitting needles that are held parallel. Cut yarn, leaving about a 18-inch (46-cm) end. Thread the end through a tapestry needle. Working from right to left, * insert tapestry needle into first stitch on front needle as if to knit and slip stitch off needle. Insert tapestry needle into next stitch on front needle as if to purl and leave on needle. Insert tapestry needle into first stitch on back knitting needle as if to purl and slip stitch off needle. Insert tapestry needle into next stitch on back needle as if to knit and leave on needle.* Repeat from * to * until all stitches are woven in. Fasten off yarn.

Kitchener Stitch

■ STITCH GUIDE

Stockinette Stitch (worked in rounds)
Round 1 (and all other rounds): (right side) Knit.

Stockinette Stitch (worked in rows)
Row 1: (right side) Knit.
            Row 2: Purl.
            Repeat Rows 1 and 2 for pattern.

2 × 2 Rib (worked in rounds over a multiple of 4 stitches)
    Round 1 (and all other rounds): *Knit 2, purl 2*.
    Repeat from * to * around.

Heel Stitch (worked in rows)
    Row 1: (wrong side) Slip first stitch as if to purl. Purl across row.
    Row 2: (right side) *Slip 1 stitch as if to purl, knit 1.* Repeat
        from * to * across row.

Note: See pages 36–37 for notes on the striping sequences used in the samples. Follow as you wish or create your own stripes.

■ BASIC SOCKS

Using one double-pointed needle, cast on 48 stitches. Divide these stitches evenly onto 3 double-pointed needles so that there are 16 stitches on each needle. Join into a round, being careful not to twist stitches. (See page 31 on working with circular and double-pointed needles.) Work 1½" (3.8 cm) in 2 × 2 Rib. Change to stockinette stitch and work even until cuff measures a total length of 6 (7)" (15 [18] cm) or desired length.

■ DIVIDE FOR HEEL FLAP

At this point you are going to switch from working in rounds to working back and forth in rows, but only on half of the total number of stitches. In addition

Variation I: 21 stitches and 30 rows (rounds) = 4" (10 cm) in stockinette stitch on size 3 (3.25 mm) needles; Variation II: 23 stitches and 34 rows = 4" (10 cm). *Note:* You can use the same number of stitches for both the men's and women's socks by taking advantage of the difference in gauge to create a larger and smaller size.

Try some other striping sequences

to this, you'll have to adjust the stitches so that the beginning and end of the round is located at the center back of the sock. So, knit the first 12 stitches of the next round. Slip the remaining 4 stitches on to the second needle, then slip the first 4 stitches of the third needle back to the second needle so that there are now 24 stitches on the second needle (instep stitches) and 12 stitches on both the first and third needles. Now slip the 12 stitches from the third needle on to the first needle so that only two needles have 24 stitches each and your yarn is at the end of the first needle and the beginning and end point of your round is at the center of this needle. At this point you will be working with these stitches only and the second needle will be acting as a temporary stitch holder. Turn work (just simply turn your work around as if you finished the row) and work Row 1 of heel-flap stitch (slip first stitch as if to purl, purl remaining stitches). Continue working these 24 stitches in heel-flap stitch until flap measures 2¼" (5.5 cm), ending with a Row 2.

■ TURN HEEL:

Purl across first 12 stitches plus 2 more stitches—14 stitches total. Purl next 2 stitches together. Purl 1 more stitch. Turn work. Slip first stitch as if to purl. Knit 5. Slip next 2 stitches, one at a time, to right-hand needle as if to knit. Insert left-hand needle from left to right into the front of these 2 stitches and knit them together (see page 23)—this will be referred to as SSK from here on. Knit 1. Turn work. Slip first stitch as if to purl. Purl 6. Purl next 2 stitches together. Purl 1. Turn work. Slip first stitch as if to purl. Knit next 7 stitches. SSK. Knit 1. Turn work. Continue working as established, knitting or purling 1 more stitch each row as indicated until all stitches have been worked, ending with a knit row—14 stitches remain. To make sure you are doing this correctly, when you decrease (either by purling 2 stitches together or SSK) you will be closing an apparent gap between 2 stitches. You are now ready to change back to working in rounds. With right side of work facing

and spare needle, pick up 12 stitches evenly along side of heel flap. Knit across 24 instep stitches, then pick up 12 stitches evenly along other side of heel flap. Knit across 7 stitches from bottom of heel. Knit remaining 7 stitches on to first needle. You should have a total of 62 stitches with 19 stitches on first needle, 24 stitches on second needle, and 19 stitches on third needle. Work 1 round even.

▪ DECREASE FOR FOOT

You now begin the final part of our heel shaping which will also return you to the original number of 48 stitches. On next round, knit to last 3 stitches on first needle, knit 2 together, knit 1. Knit across 24 instep stitches. On third needle knit 1, SSK, knit to end. Work 1 round even. Repeat these 2 rounds until 48 stitches remain with 12 stitches each on first and third needles and 24 stitches on second (instep) needle. Work even until foot is 2" (5 cm) shorter than desired total length.

▪ DECREASE FOR TOE

On next round knit to last 3 stitches on first needle, knit 2 stitches together, knit 1. On second needle knit 1, SSK, knit to last 3 stitches, knit 2 together, knit 1. On third needle, knit 1, SSK, knit to end. Work 1 round even. Repeat these 2 rounds until 5 stitches remain on both first and third needles and 10 stitches remain on second needle. With third needle, knit across stitches from first needle so that there are 10 stitches each on 2 needles and yarn is at end of 1 needle. Cut yarn, leaving an 18" (46 cm) tail. Work kitchener stitch (see page 34) to join toe stitches together invisibly. Weave in loose ends.

▪ STRIPE SEQUENCES FOR VARIATION I

Heel flap for both socks is worked alternating 2 rows each color C and A starting with color C for a total of 20 rows. Heel turning for both socks is worked in color C. Both socks pick up stitches with color D and alternate 2 rounds each B and D until heel decreases are completed for total of 16 rounds.

Sock 1	Sock 2
Rib -	Rib -
12 rounds A	12 rounds A
Cuff (38 rounds total)	
2 rounds C	2 rounds C
4 rounds B	8 rounds B
4 rounds A	8 rounds A
4 rounds B	4 rounds C
4 rounds D	8 rounds A
4 rounds B	8 rounds B
4 rounds C	
4 rounds B	
4 rounds A	
4 rounds B	

Foot Stripes (42 rounds total)

Toe decreases for both socks are worked alternating 2 rounds each C and A for a total of 14 rounds beginning with C.

	Sock 1	Sock 2
	4 rounds D	4 rounds D
	8 rounds B	4 rounds B
	8 rounds A	4 rounds A
	4 rounds C	4 rounds B
	8 rounds A	4 rounds C
	8 rounds B	4 rounds B
	2 rounds D	4 rounds D
		4 rounds B
		4 rounds A
		4 rounds B
		2 rounds D

■ **STRIPE SEQUENCES FOR VARIATION II**

Rib—(Same for both socks) cast on with D. Work a total of 10 rounds, alternating 2 rounds each, D and B.

	Sock 1	Sock 2
	Cuff (38 rounds total)	
	2 rounds A	4 rounds A
	2 rounds C	6 rounds C
	2 rounds A	6 rounds B
	2 rounds C	6 rounds C
	2 rounds B	2 rounds A
	2 rounds C	2 rounds D
	4 rounds B	2 rounds A
	2 rounds D	2 rounds B
	2 rounds B	2 rounds A
	6 rounds A	2 rounds C
	4 rounds D	4 rounds A
	8 rounds C	

Heel flap for both socks is worked alternating 2 rows each color C and B starting with color C and working a total of 20 rows. Heel turning for both socks is worked in color B. Both socks pick up stitches with color D. Remainder of foot, including heel decreases is worked as follows at right (52 rounds total).

Toe decreases for both socks are worked alternating 2 rounds each color C and B beginning with color C and working a total of 14 rounds.

	Sock 1	Sock 2
	2 rounds D	2 rounds D
	2 rounds A	2 rounds A
	2 rounds D	2 rounds D
	2 rounds C	2 rounds A
	2 rounds A	2 rounds D
	2 rounds B	2 rounds C
	2 rounds C	2 rounds D
	2 rounds A	2 rounds C
	4 rounds D	4 rounds B
	6 rounds B	2 rounds A
	8 rounds C	2 rounds B
	6 rounds B	6 rounds A
	4 rounds A	4 rounds C
	2 rounds C	8 rounds D
	6 rounds D	6 rounds B
		2 rounds A
		2 rounds D

MEASURING FOR A CUSTOM FIT

Although most sock patterns are estimated to fit the average foot, it is easy to adjust for any extremes in length. Socks are measured from heel tip to toe tip (A). When you are knitting, allow 2" (5 cm) for toe decreasing on adult's socks and 1½" (3.8 cm) for children's socks (B). Therefore, if you are measuring a foot, or a well-fitting pair of existing socks, subtract the proper measurement for the toe from the total length. Socks are one garment for which we do not allow extra width or length for ease. It is better to err on the small side because most socks will stretch to conform to the foot. Cuffs are also easily adjusted. Measure from the ankle upward to the desired height (C). Cuff length for ankle socks is 4–8" (10 –20.5 cm) for women (average 6" [15 cm]) and 6–8" (15–20.5 cm) for men (average 7" [18 cm]).

Note: These measurements do not apply to knee socks that require more complex measurements and shaping to accommodate the calf. In general, the width for both the cuff and foot are the same. This measurement is easily adjusted to fit a wider foot or heavier calf. It is best to work with an even number of stitches. Measure around the widest part and multiply by the stitch gauge. If the foot is wider than the calf, work fewer decreases after heel turning; if the calf is wider than the foot, work more decreases after heel turning.

INNER CHILD
MITTENS

Mittens have a way of transporting us back in time—a time when snow meant skating, snowmen, and fort building. So slip these on, go outside, and enjoy the winter wonderland. Snowboarding, anyone? Whether knitted on two or four needles, these mittens work up quickly.

■ SIZE	■ YARN	■ NEEDLES	■ NOTIONS	■ GAUGE
To fit an average adult hand. Finished mitten is about 10½" (26.5 cm) long and 4½" (11.5 cm) wide.	Worsted-weight yarn, about 175 yd (160 m). We used Brown Sheep Wool Lamb's Pride Worsted (85% wool, 15% mohair; 190 yards [174 m]/4 oz): 1 skein, #M180 ruby red.	Ribbing—Size 6 (4 mm). Hand—Size 8 (5 mm). Adjust needle size if necessary to obtain the correct gauge.	Tapestry needle; stitch markers; two stitch holders about 4½" (11.5 cm) long.	18 stitches and 24 rows = 4" (10 cm) in stockinette stitch on size 8 (5 mm) needles.

TWO-NEEDLE MITTENS

■ **STITCH GUIDE**

1 × 1 Rib (worked in rows over an even number of stitches)
Row 1: *Knit 1, purl 1*. Repeat from * to * across row.
Repeat this row for pattern.

Stockinette Stitch (worked in rows)
Row 1: (right side) Knit all stitches.
Row 2: Purl all stitches.
Repeat Rows 1 and 2 for pattern.

■ **MITTENS**

With smaller needles, cast on 34 stitches. Work 2½" (6.5 cm) in 1 × 1 rib, increasing 6 stitches evenly across last row—40 stitches. Change to larger needles and stockinette stitch and work 6 rows even, ending with a wrong-side row. *Shape thumb gusset* (see page 43): On next row knit 18, place marker on needle, increase in next stitch by knitting into front and back of stitch (see Basics, page 91), knit next 2 stitches, increase in next stitch as before, place a second marker on needle, knit 18. Purl 1 row. On next row knit to marker, slip marker, increase in next stitch, knit to stitch before marker, increase in next stitch, slip marker, knit to end. Purl 1 row. Repeat last 2 rows until there are 12 stitches between markers. Work 5 rows even, ending with a wrong-side row.

THUMB

On next row, knit 18 stitches and place on holder. Knit across 12 thumb stitches. Place remaining 18 stitches on second holder. Turn work. Cast on 2 stitches. Purl across these 2 stitches and the 12 thumb stitches. Turn work. Cast on 2 stitches and knit across all 16 stitches. Work even in stockinette stitch on 16 stitches until thumb measures 1½" (3.8 cm) or 1" (2.5 cm) less than desired length, ending with a wrong-side row. *Shape thumb top:* On next row * knit 2, knit 2 together*. Repeat from * to * across row—12 stitches remain in thumb. Purl 1 row. On next row *knit 1, knit 2 together*. Repeat from * to * across row—8 stitches remain. Purl 1 row. Knit 2 together across next row. Cut yarn, leaving a tail about 12" (30.5 cm) long. Using a tapestry needle, thread tail through remaining 4 stitches, pull tight closing thumb top (see page 30), and fasten off. Use remainder of tail to sew thumb seam using mattress stitch (see Basics, page 92). Weave in loose ends to wrong side of work and secure.

HAND

With right side of work facing, join yarn at base of thumb (bend thumb forward) and pick up (see page 47) and knit 4 stitches in cast on thumb stitches. Place 18 stitches from second stitch holder on needle and knit. Turn and purl across 22 stitches. Place 18 stitches from first stitch holder on needle and purl across. Work even in stockinette stitch on 40 stitches until work measures 9 ½" (24 cm) ending with a wrong-side row. *Shape top:* *Knit 2, knit 2 together*. Repeat from * to * across row— 30 stitches remain. Purl 1 row. On next row *knit 1, knit 2 together*. Repeat from * to * across row—20 stitches remain. Purl 1 row. Knit 2 together across next row. Cut yarn, leaving a tail about 18" (46 cm) long. Using a tapestry needle, thread tail through remaining 10 stitches (see page 30), pull tight closing mitten top, and fasten off. Use remainder of tail to sew mitten seam using mattress stitch. Weave in loose ends to wrong side of work and secure.

■ SIZE	■ YARN	■ NEEDLES	■ NOTIONS	■ GAUGE
To fit average adult hand. Finished mitten is about 10 ½" (26.5 cm) long and 4 ½" (11.5 cm) wide.	Worsted-weight yarn, about 90 yd (83 m) each of two colors. We used Rowan Kid Soft (35% extra fine merino wool, 40% kid mohair, 25% nylon; 135 yd [125 m]/50 g): 1 ball each # 759 soft blue (A) and #757 black (B).	Size 4 (3.5 mm) and 6 (4 mm): set of 4 double-pointed needles. Adjust needle size if necessary to obtain the correct gauge.	Tapestry needle; stitch markers; stitch holder.	16 stitches and 24 rows = 4" (10 cm) in circular stockinette stitch on size 6 (4mm) needles.

FOUR-NEEDLE MITTENS

■ STITCH GUIDE

1 × 1 Rib (worked in rounds over an even number of stitches)
Row 1: *Knit 1, purl 1*. Repeat from * to * across round. Repeat this round for pattern.

Stockinette Stitch (worked in rounds)
Round 1 (and all other rounds): (right side) Knit all stitches.

■ MITTENS

With smaller needles and color B, cast on 30 stitches (see circular knitting, page 31). Divide stitches evenly among 3 needles. Join, being careful not to twist stitches. Work in 1 × 1 rib until piece measures 1¼" (3.2 cm). Change to color A (see page 6), and continue in rib for an additional 1¼" (3.2 cm), increasing 6 stitches evenly in last round—36 stitches. Knit 1 round. Change to larger needles, stockinette stitch, and color B, and work 6 rounds even alternating colors every 2 rounds. On last round, place markers as follows: knit 16, place marker on needle, knit 4, place second marker on needle, knit 16. *Shape thumb gusset:* *Keeping in stripe pattern as established, on next round knit to marker, slip marker and increase in next stitch by knitting into the front and back of the stitch (see Basics, page 91). Knit to stitch before next marker, increase in next stitch as before, slip marker and knit to end of round. Work 1 round even.* Repeat from * to * until there are 12 stitches between markers. Work 5 rounds even. On next round, knit to second marker. Place 12 thumb stitches between markers on a holder and work to end of round. On next round, cast on 4 stitches over space from thumb stitches. Work even in stripe pattern until work measures 8½" (21.5 cm) total length. Work even for 1" (2.5 cm) more alternating stripes every round. When work measures 9½" (24 cm), *shape top:* On next round **knit 2, knit 2 together**. Repeat from ** to ** across round—27 stitches remain. Work 1 round even. On next round **Knit 1, knit 2 together**—18 stitches remain. Repeat from ** to ** across round. Work 1 round even. On next round knit 2 together around—9 stitches remain. Knit 1 more round. Cut yarn, leaving a tail about 8" (20.5 cm) long. Using a tapestry needle, thread tail through remaining stitches (see page 30), pull tight to close mitten top, and fasten off.

■ **THUMB:**

With larger needles and color B, place 12 stitches from stitch holder back on needle and pick up (see page 47) 4 stitches where the 4 stitches were cast on for the body. Divide these 16 stitches evenly on 3 needles. Work 1¼" (3.2 cm). Change to color A and work an additional ¾" (2 cm). *Shape top:* On next round, **knit 1, knit 2 together**. Repeat from ** to ** around, end knit 1—11 stitches remain. Knit 1 round. On next round, knit 2 together around, end knit 1. Knit 1 round. Cut yarn, leaving a tail about 6" (15 cm) long. Using a tapestry needle, thread tail through remaining 6 stitches, pull tight to close thumb top, and fasten off. Weave in loose ends to wrong side of work and secure.

THUMB GUSSET

When you're increasing throughout the body of a garment, the increases are usually evenly spread out and become hidden in the garment, barely noticeable. Conversely, for a thumb gusset, the designated thumb increases are concentrated in a specific area. As you repeatedly increase in the same stitch on subsequent rows, adding the new stitches in between markers, eventually that area appears to move in a different direction from the rest of the body, and the mitten begins to conform to the shape of the hand. The gusset stitches move outward while the rest of the stitches stay straight.

When enough stitches have been increased to form a thumb, the designated stitches are isolated even further and knitted separately as thumb stitches. Taken step by step, this procedure is not at all difficult, yet the graceful shaping it creates looks much more complex.

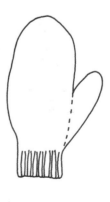

RIBBED
RIBBON TANK

Ribbing makes this tank top form-fitting and body-hugging—definitely not cling-free. Graceful, subtle shaping is achieved by varying the needle size, bringing in the top at the waist and back out again.

SIZE

34 (36, 38, 40, 42)" (86.5 [91.5, 96.5, 101.5, 106.5] cm) bust/chest circumference. Sweater shown measures 36" (91.5 cm).

YARN

Worsted- to light bulky-weight ribbon yarn, about 575 (600, 625, 650, 675) yd [527 (550, 575, 595, 618] m]. We used Trendsetter Dolcino (75% acrylic myolis, 25% polyamide; 99 yd [90 m]/ 50 g): 6 (6, 7, 7, 7) skeins # 109 chartreuse.

NEEDLES

Body—Size 8 (5mm), 9 (5.5 mm) and 10 (6 mm). Neckline—Size 8 (5 mm) 24" (60-cm) circular needles. Adjust needle size if necessary to obtain the correct gauge.

NOTIONS

Tapestry needle; sixteen safety pins or short pieces of contrasting yarn for marking edges; two stitch markers; crochet hook (optional) size F or smaller for picking up stitches.

GAUGE

16 stitches and 20 rows = 4" (10 cm) in stockinette stitch on size 10 (6 mm) needles. 16.5 stitches and 24 rows = 4" (10 cm) in 2 × 2 rib (slightly stretched) on size 10 (6 mm) needles.

STITCH GUIDE

2 × 2 Rib (worked over a multiple of 4 stitches + 2)
Row 1: (right side) *Knit 2, purl 2*. Repeat from * to * across row, end knit 2.
Row 2: *Purl 2, knit 2*. Repeat from * to * across row, end purl 2.
Repeat Rows 1 and 2 for pattern.

BACK AND FRONT

With size 10 (6 mm) needles, cast on 70 (74, 78, 82, 86) stitches. Work in 2 × 2 rib until piece measures 2 (2, 2, 3, 3)" (5 [5, 5, 7.5, 7.5] cm). Mark edge with safety pin or contrast yarn and change to size 9 (5.5 mm) needles. Continue in pattern as established for another 2" (5 cm). Mark edge as before and change to size 8 (5mm) needles, working another 4" (10 cm) in pattern. Mark edge and change to size 9 (5.5 mm) needles. Work 2" (5 cm) even. Mark edge. Change to size 10 (6 mm) needles and work even in pattern until piece measures 13 (14, 14, 15, 15)" (33 [35.5, 35.5, 38, 38] cm) from beginning; end with a wrong-side row. *Shape armhole:* Bind off 4 stitches at beginning of next 2 rows, then decrease 1 stitch each armhole edge every other row 6 (8, 10, 10, 10) times, working decreases as follows: on right-side rows, knit 1, ssk, (see page 23) work to last 3 stitches, knit 2 together, knit 1; on wrong-side rows, work stitches as they appear. *At the same time,* when armhole measures 2 (2, 2½, 3, 3)" (5 [5, 6.5, 7.5, 7.5] cm), *shape neck:* (see page 47) place markers either side of center 10 stitches. Work to first marker, join new ball of yarn and bind off center 10 stitches, work to end of row. Working each side of neck with a separate ball of yarn, and maintaining stitch pattern, bind off at each side of neck edge 3 stitches once, 2 stitches 2 times, then 1 stitch 3 (3, 3, 4, 5) times. When armhole measures 7 (7, 7½, 8, 8)" (18 [18, 19, 20.5, 20.5] cm), bind off at each shoulder edge 5 stitches 2 (2, 2, 1, 0) time(s), then 6 stitches 0 (0, 0, 1, 2) time(s). Make front to match back.

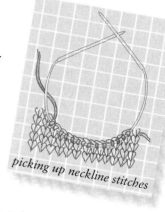

picking up neckline stitches

Schematic (Front & Back)

7 (7, 7, 7¾, 8)"
18 (18, 18, 19.5, 20.5) cm

2½" (2½, 2½, 2⅔, 3)"
6.5 (6.5, 6.5, 6.65, 7.5) cm

¼"
6 mm

5¼"
13.5 cm

7 (7, 7½, 8, 8)"
18 (18, 19, 20.5, 20.5) cm

13 (14, 14, 15, 15)"
33 (35.5, 35.5, 38, 38) cm

**FRONT &
BACK**

17 (18, 19, 20, 21)" 43 (46, 48.5, 51, 53.5) cm

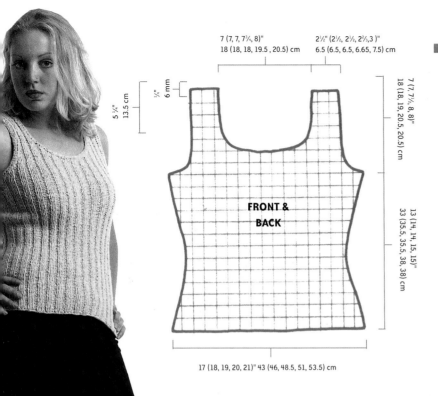

■ **FINISHING**

With right sides together, sew shoulder seams using a backstitch (see Basics, page 92). *Armhole edges:* With right side of work facing and size 8 (5 mm) needles, pick up along each armhole edge 68 (68, 72, 76, 76) stitches. Knit 1 row. Bind off all stitches. Using mattress stitch (see Basics, page 92), align side edge markers together and sew side seams. Remove markers. With size 8 (5 mm) circular needle and right side of work facing, beginning at shoulder seam, pick up 128 (128, 132, 136, 136) stitches evenly around neck edge. Join and purl 1 row. Bind off all stitches. Weave in loose ends.

RIBBING has two main functions in knitting. First, it's an "elastic" stitch so a number of stitches knitted in a rib stitch will create a narrower but stretchier fabric than the same number knitted in, say, stockinette stitch. Ribbing is used at the edges of garments both to keep them from stretching out and, in the most basic sense, to keep warmth in. Second, ribbing creates a balanced, reversible fabric. Since there are the same or similar number of knit and purl stitches on either side of the work, ribbing will not curl as stockinette stitch does, another good reason to use ribbing at garment edges.

When ribbing is used for a full garment rather than just as an edge finish, it can create a fitted, body-hugging garment which needs no additional shaping—the elasticity of the fabric allows it to be shaped by the body. Further subtle shaping can be achieved by adjustments in needle size. Working parts of the garment in needles one or two sizes larger or smaller than the main needle size will widen or narrow the garment without breaking the line of the rib.

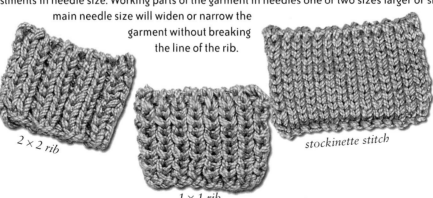

2 × 2 rib

1 × 1 rib

stockinette stitch

When you're **SHAPING A NECKLINE** there comes a point where the work must be separated in order to knit each side of the neck and shoulder. Some patterns will say to work one side at a time while others will direct you to attach a new yarn and work each side at the same time (Figure 1 & 2). Although either method will work and the choice is ultimately one of personal preference, working each side at the same time with a separate ball of yarn will ensure the same number of rows on each side.

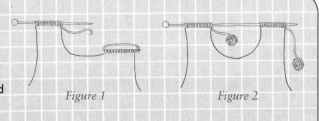

Figure 1   *Figure 2*

When the pattern directs you to **JOIN A NEW YARN**, simply stop using the ball you are working with, take a second ball and secure it to your work with a simple knot that can be untied later (Figure 3); then continue to work as directed with the new yarn. On the next row, work to the neck opening, stop using the new ball and pick up the first one and work to the end (Figure 4). Keep in mind that the neck and shoulder shaping will be a mirror image on each side. Also, while you can work decreases in the same row, bind offs can only occur at the beginning of a row so they will alternate rows on either side of the neck edge.

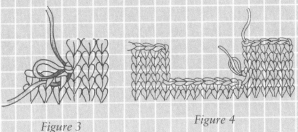

Figure 3   *Figure 4*

When you're **PICKING UP STITCHES**, whether for a neck edge or a front edge, you not only finish that edge but also stabilize it and define the finished measurement. Concealing the raw edge and spacing the stitches evenly are of top importance. Here's how you do it. With the right side of the work facing, temporarily anchor yarn at right-hand edge (tie a half knot you can untie later) and with a knitting needle or crochet hook in right hand, go under both sides of edge or bound-off stitch and pull through a loop of yarn. Place loop on needle in right hand—one stitch picked up (Figure 1). ***Note:*** Some people prefer to use a crochet hook because it is easier to grab the yarn and pull it through and then place the loop on the knitting needle. Other people find it easier to work directly with the knitting needle. Trial

and error will determine the most comfortable method for you. Continue in this manner until the total number of loops are on your needle. Treat these as stitches and knit or purl them as directed [Figure 2]. Because some patterns tell you exactly how many stitches to pick up in a given area, it is easy to space stitches evenly. Other patterns just indicate a total number of stitches. In the latter case, divide the length or circumference into quarters and pick up 25% of the total stitches in each quarter. The spacing of the first quarter will generally give you a guideline for spacing.

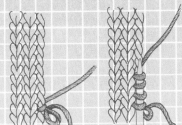

Figure 1   *Figure 2*

HELPFUL TIPS:

On a front band, remember to keep first and last stitches as close to upper and lower edge as possible unless otherwise indicated.

When you're picking up stitches along a curved bound-off edge, such as a neck edge, ignore the "jogs" and treat the edge as one smooth line, drawing spaces together.

When you're picking up stitches along a straight horizontal edge, you can generally pick up one stitch in each stitch, but along a vertical edge you will need to skip stitches to avoid a ruffled edge. For example, at a gauge of 4 stitches and 6 rows per inch, you would pick up 4 stitches out of 6 to keep the edge even.

NO SLEEVES
FUNNEL TOP

Maybe this should be called the lightning speed top—it's that fast. In addition to the speed in using the super chunky yarn or knitting multiple strands of lightweight yarn together, this top is further simplified by having the edge finishing built right in to the knitting. Once the knitting is completed, all that's needed is some simple seaming.

■ SIZE

34 (36, 39, 41, 43)" (86.5 [91.5, 99, 104, 109] cm) bust/chest circumference. Sweater shown measures 36" (91.5 cm).

■ YARN

Single-strand version: Super chunky-weight yarn, about 280 (300, 350, 375, 400) yd (256 [275, 320, 344, 366] m). We used Classic Elite Weekend Cotton (100% mercerized cotton; 51 yd [47 m]/100 g): 6 (6, 7, 8, 8) skeins, #4085 berries.

Multi-strand version: Worsted-weight yarn, about 280 (300, 350, 375, 400) yd (256, [275, 320, 344, 366] m) each of three different colors.

We used Mission Falls 1824 Cotton (100% cotton; 84 yards [77 m]/50 g): 4 (4, 5, 5, 5) skeins each of # 300 lichen, #104 sand, #204 lentil. Work with one strand of each color held together as one yarn.

■ NEEDLES

Size 13 (9mm). Adjust needle size if necessary to obtain the correct gauge.

■ NOTIONS

Tapestry needle.

■ GAUGE

9 stitches and 12 rows = 4" (10 cm) in stockinette stitch on size 13 (9 mm) needles with either one strand of super chunky yarn or 3 strands of worsted-weight yarn.

■ STITCH GUIDE

Garter Stitch
Knit all rows.

Stockinette Stitch
Row 1: (right side) Knit all stitches.
Row 2: Purl all stitches.
Repeat Rows 1 and 2 for pattern.

CLOSED BOTTOM VERSION

■ BACK AND FRONT

Cast on 38 (40, 44, 46, 48) stitches. Work garter stitch for 3 rows. Beginning with Row 1, change to stockinette stitch and work even until piece measures 11½, (12, 12, 12½, 13)" (29 [30.5, 30.5, 31.5, 33] cm) from cast-on edge, ending with a wrong-side row. *Shape armholes:* Bind off 2 stitches at beginning of next 2 rows, then decrease 1 stitch each edge every other row 3 (3, 5, 5, 6) times, working decreases as follows: on *right-side rows*, knit 2, ssk, (see page 23), knit to last 4 stitches, knit 2 together, knit 2; on *wrong-side rows*, knit 2, purl to last 2 stitches, knit 2. Continue on remaining 28 (30, 30, 32, 32) stitches, working 2 stitches at each edge in garter stitch and remaining stitches in stockinette stitch until armhole measures 7½, (7½, 8, 8, 8)" (19 [19, 20.5, 20.5, 20.5] cm). *Shape neck and shoulders:* Bind off 2 (3, 3, 3, 3) stitches at beginning of next 2 rows, then 2 (2, 2, 2, 2) stitches at beginning of next 2 rows. Work even on remaining 20 (20, 20, 22, 22) stitches for 2" (5 cm). Knit 2 rows. Bind off loosely. Make front to match back.

Use three yarns together

SIDE SLIT BOTTOM VERSION

■ **BACK AND FRONT**

Cast on 38 (40, 44, 46, 48) stitches. Work garter stitch for 3 rows. Work edge slits as follows: On *right-side rows*, knit all stitches. On *wrong-side rows*, knit 2, purl to last 2 stitches, knit 2. When work measures 3" (7.5 cm) from beginning, change to all stockinette stitch and follow instructions for Closed Bottom Version.

■ **FINISHING**

Sew the neck and shoulder seams all in one seam using the mattress stitch for neck and backstitch (see Basics, page 92) for shoulder. Sew side seams using mattress stitch. Weave in loose ends.

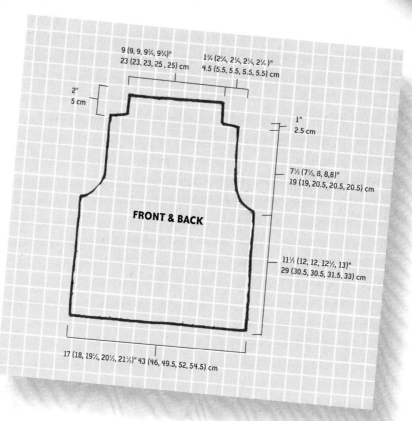

9 (9, 9, 9¼, 9¾)"
23 (23, 23, 25 , 25) cm

1¾ (2¼, 2¼, 2¼, 2¼)"
4.5 (5.5, 5.5, 5.5, 5.5) cm

2"
5 cm

1"
2.5 cm

7½ (7½, 8, 8,8)"
19 (19, 20.5, 20.5, 20.5) cm

FRONT & BACK

11½ (12, 12, 12½, 13)"
29 (30.5, 30.5, 31.5, 33) cm

17 (18, 19¼, 20½, 21½)" 43 (46, 49.5, 52, 54.5) cm

COMBINING YARNS

Multiple strands of yarn held together and knitted as one yarn can be a fun and challenging way of to create one-of-a-kind textures and colors. A key to success, though, is to swatch and experiment with colors and textures, since, very often, three or four yarns that look perfect when held side by side can turn disastrous when knitted together. Color can change dramatically when mixed. If one yarn used is multicolored, keep in mind that like colors pulled from that yarn will cancel each other out. On the other hand, the higher the contrast between colors, the busier the resulting fabric will appear. It is far easier to start out mixing tones or textures of one color and slowly adding other colors until you reach an effect that pleases you. Also, consider adding a contrast yarn like a matte, shiny, or metallic.

Needle size can make a difference in the fabric created. Be sure to swatch on several different sizes because there is no easy formula to predict appropriate needle size. Moreover, multiple yarns can often cancel out texture, especially if the needle used is too small.

Keep fiber compatibility in mind. It is perfectly fine to mix fibers, but consider how the garment will ultimately be cared for. If you are planning to dry clean there are few limitations. If you plan to hand or machine wash, check that all the fibers will react in the same way. It is a good idea to wash swatches before beginning a garment.

When you're determining yarn quantities for your project, keep in mind that you will need to purchase sufficient yardage for each color. If the pattern calls for 500 yards (457 meters) of chunky yarn, you will need to purchase 500 yards (457 meters) each of all the yarns used in your mix.

Keeping these tips in mind, the more you experiment the stronger your mixing skills will become, and they will offer you the opportunity to create individualized and painterly fabrics.

ROLLOVER
PULLOVER

This pullover is one you could live in for years. The drop shoulders, softly-rolled neckline, and simple construction make it perfect for a "first sweater."

■ SIZE

40 (44, 48, 50, 52)" (101.5, [112, 122, 127, 132] cm) bust/chest circumference. 23 (24, 25, 25, 26)" (58.5 [61, 63.5, 63.5, 66] cm) long. Sizes are unisex. Add 2" (5 cm) in sleeve length for a man's version. If you like an oversized sweater, choose a size that's at least 6" (15 cm) larger than your bust/chest circumference. Sweater shown measures 48" (122 cm).

■ YARN

Bulky-weight yarn, about 650 (700, 750, 800, 850) yd (594 [640, 685, 732, 777] m). We used Tahki Soho Tweed (100% wool; 110 yd [100 m]/100 g): 6 (7, 7, 8, 8) skeins, #302 beige tweed.

■ NEEDLES

Edges—Size 9 (5.5 mm). Body— Size 10½ (6.5 mm). Neckline— Size 9 (5.5 mm): 16" (40-cm) circular needle. Adjust needle size if necessary to obtain the correct gauge.

■ NOTIONS

Tapestry needle; safety pins for markers; four stitch holders about 6" (15 cm) long.

■ GAUGE

13 stitches and 20 rows = 4" (10 cm) in stockinette stitch on size 10½ (6.5 mm) needles.

■ STITCH GUIDE

Stockinette Stitch
Row 1: (right side) Knit all stitches.
Row 2: Purl all stitches.
Repeat Rows 1 and 2 for pattern.

Garter Stitch
Knit all rows.

■ BACK

With edging needles, cast on 64 (70, 76, 80, 84) stitches. Work 1" (2.5 cm) in garter stitch, ending with a wrong-side row. Change to body needles and stockinette stitch and work even until piece measures 23 (24, 25, 25, 26)" (58.5 [61, 63.5, 63.5, 66] cm) from cast-on edge, ending with a wrong-side row. On next row (right side), knit across first 21 (24, 26, 27, 29) stitches and place on stitch holder. Bind off next 22 (22, 24, 26, 26) stitches. Work across remaining 21 (24, 26, 27, 29) stitches and place on second stitch holder. Cut yarn.

■ FRONT

Work as for back until piece measures 19½ (20½, 21½, 21½, 22½)" (49.5 [52, 54.5, 54.5, 57] cm), ending with a wrong-side row. *Shape neck:* Knit across 29 (32, 34, 36, 38) stitches, join new yarn and bind off center 6 (6, 8, 8, 8) stitches, knit to end of row. Working each side of neck with a separate ball of yarn, bind off at each side of neck edge 3 stitches once, 2 stitches once, then 1 stitch 3 (3, 3, 4, 4) times. Work even until piece measures same as back, place remaining 21 (24, 26, 27, 29) stitches each side on stitch holders. Cut yarn.

What about a soft chenille?

Here's a great slubby yarn.

KNITTING SHOULDERS TOGETHER

Bind off and join the shoulder seams all at one time. This method creates a neat and sturdy seam with little added bulk. It is ideal for straight horizontal seams, such as dropped shoulders, when both sides of the seam have the same number of stitches. It may seem awkward at first, but it's easy to learn with a little practice and the professional result is worth the effort.

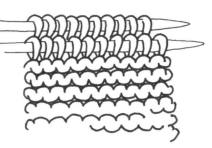

Figure 1

Slip shoulder stitches from right-hand side of back onto an empty needle. Repeat for stitches from right-hand side of front. Hold work with right sides together and both needles parallel in left hand (Figure 1). Attach yarn and with a third needle knit the first stitch from each needle together as one (Figure 2). Repeat with next stitch from each needle. You now have two stitches on right-hand needle. Bind off one stitch using the tip of one left-hand needle to take the first stitch on right-hand needle over the second (Figure 3). Knit next two stitches together from left-hand needles the same way and repeat bind-off. Repeat across row until all stitches are bound off. Cut yarn and pull tail through last stitch.

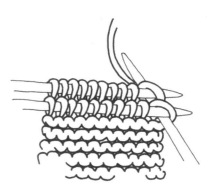

Figure 2

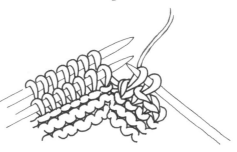

Figure 3

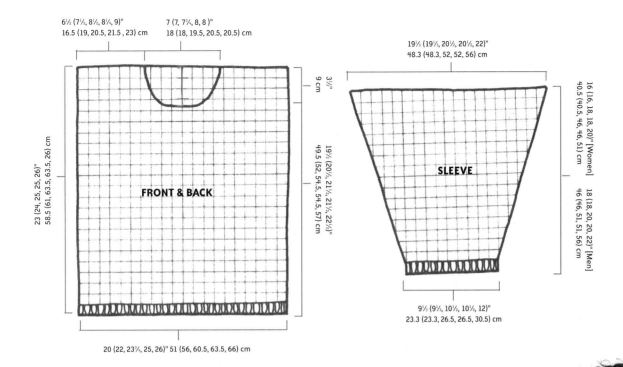

FRONT & BACK

6½ (7½, 8½, 8¼, 9)"
16.5 (19, 20.5, 21.5, 23) cm

7 (7, 7¾, 8, 8)"
18 (18, 19.5, 20.5, 20.5) cm

3½"
9 cm

23 (24, 25, 25, 26)"
58.5 (61, 63.5, 63.5, 66) cm

19½ (20½, 21¼, 21½, 22½)"
49.5 (52, 54.5, 54.5, 57) cm

20 (22, 23¾, 25, 26)" 51 (56, 60.5, 63.5, 66) cm

SLEEVE

19½ (19½, 20½, 20½, 22)"
48.3 (48.3, 52, 52, 56) cm

16 (16, 18, 18, 20)" [Women]
40.5 (40.5, 46, 46, 51) cm

18 (18, 20, 20, 22)" [Men]
46 (46, 51, 51, 56) cm

9⅓ (9⅓, 10½, 10½, 12)"
23.3 (23.3, 26.5, 26.5, 30.5) cm

SLEEVES

With edging needles, cast on 30 (30, 34, 34, 38) stitches. Work 1" (2.5 cm) in garter stitch, ending with a wrong-side row. Change to body needles and stockinette stitch increasing 1 stitch each end of needle every 4 rows 10 (10, 8, 8, 6) times, then every 6 rows 6 (6, 8, 8, 10) times—62 (62, 66, 66, 70) stitches. Work even until piece measures 16 (16, 18, 18, 20)" (40.5 [40.5, 46, 46, 51] cm) or 18 (18, 20, 20, 22)" (46 [46, 51, 51, 56] cm) for men's sizes. Bind off all stitches.

FINISHING

Block all pieces to correct measurements. Knit shoulders together. *Neckband:* With circular needle, right-side facing, pick up 60 (60, 64, 66, 66) stitches evenly around neck edge (see page 47). Work in stockinette stitch until neckband measures 2" (5 cm). Bind off all stitches. *Seaming:* Measure down from shoulder seam 10 (10, 10½, 10½, 11)" (25.5 [25.5, 26.5, 26.5, 28] cm) along sides of both front and back and mark with safety pins or scraps of contrasting yarn. With right sides together, position bound off edge of sleeve to sides of sweater, matching center top of sleeve to shoulder seam and ends to markers. Pin in place. Using backstitch (see Basics, page 92), stitch sleeve in place. Repeat for second sleeve. Turn sweater right side out and fold along shoulder seam. Match sleeve seams at underarm and match garter stitch at sleeve edges and bottom edge. Pin in place. Using mattress stitch (see Basics, page 92) and working from right side, sew body and sleeves in one continuous seam. Repeat for second side. Weave in loose ends. Steam all seams.

A MUST-HAVE
CARDIGAN

This is an abstracted version of the basic round-neck cardigan. Rolled edges
and the absence of ribbing at the neck and front band give the sweater a soft,
contemporary feel. Because the styling is so simple, it is an ideal pattern to
show off a complex yarn, yet the sweater's simplicity can be equally striking
in a traditional yarn. Whether the cardigan is knitted close-fitting or boxy, you
need at least one.

Think of the pattern stitch possibilities...

...or use a solid color

36 (38, 40, 42, 44)" (91.5 [96.5, 101.5, 106.5, 112] cm) bust/chest circumference. 18 (19, 20, 21, 22)" (46 [48.5, 51, 53.5, 56] cm) finished length. Sweater shown measures 36" (91.5 cm).

Light bulky-weight yarn, about 810 (945) yd (740 [864] m). We used Manos Del Uruguay Kettle Dyed Wool (100% wool; 135 yd [123 m]/100 g): 6 (6, 6, 7, 7) skeins, #100 agate.

Body and Sleeves—Size 9 (5.5 mm). Neck edging— Size 7 (4 mm). Adjust needle size if necessary to obtain the correct gauge.

Tapestry needle; five buttons about ¾" (2-cm) diameter; five safety pins.

15 stitches and 20 rows = 4" (10 cm) in stockinette stitch on size 9 (5.5 mm) needles.

■ STITCH GUIDE

Stockinette Stitch
Row 1: (right side) Knit all stitches.
Row 2: Purl all stitches.
Repeat Rows 1 and 2 for pattern.

■ BACK

With larger needles, cast on 68 (72, 76, 80, 84) stitches. Work even in stockinette stitch until piece measures 11 (12, 13, 13, 14)" (28 [30.5, 33, 33, 35.5] cm) from beginning. *Shape armholes:* Bind off 4 stitches at beginning of next 2 rows, then decrease 1 stitch each edge every other row 6 (7, 8, 9, 10) times, working decreases on right-side rows as follows: knit 1, knit 2 together, knit to last 3 stitches, ssk (see page 23), knit 1. Work even on 48 (50, 52, 54, 56) stitches until piece measures 6 ½ (6 ½, 6 ½, 7 ½, 7 ½)" (16.5 [16.5, 16.5, 19, 19] cm) from beginning of armhole shaping, ending with a wrong-side row. *Shape neck and shoulders:* (RS) Knit across 15 (16, 16, 17, 17) stitches, join new yarn and bind off center 18 (18, 20, 20, 22) stitches, knit to end of row. Working each side of neck with a separate ball of yarn, bind off at each side of neck edge 2 stitches once and *at the same time* bind off at shoulder edge 6 (7, 7, 7, 7) stitches once, then 7 (7, 7, 8, 8) stitches once.

■ LEFT FRONT

With larger needles, cast on 36 (38, 40, 42, 44) stitches. Work even in stockinette stitch until piece measures 11 (12, 13, 13, 14)" (28 [30.5, 33, 33, 35.5] cm) from beginning and ending with a wrong-side row. *Shape armhole:* (right side) Bind off 4 stitches at beginning of next row. Beginning with the next right-side row, decrease 1 stitch at armhole edge every other row 6 (7, 8, 9, 10) times. Work decreases as follows: knit 1, knit 2 together,

knit across row. Work even on 26 (27, 28, 29, 30) stitches until armhole measures 3½ (3½, 3½, 4½, 4½)" (9 [9, 9, 11.5, 11.5] cm) ending with a right side row. *Shape neck:* (wrong side) Bind off at neck edge 6 stitches once, 2 stitches 2 times, then decrease 1 stitch at neck edge on every other right-side row 3 (3, 4, 4, 5) times and working decreases as follows: knit across row to last 3 stitches, knit 2 together through back loop (see page 23), knit 1. When front measures same length as back to shoulders, bind off at shoulder edge, 6 (7, 7, 7, 7) stitches once, then 7 (7, 7, 8, 8) stitches once.

■ RIGHT FRONT

Work same as for left front, reversing all shaping by binding off for armhole at beginning of a wrong-side row, and working neck shaping at beginning of right-side row. Work five buttonholes spaced as follows: Make first buttonhole 1½" (3.8 cm) from bottom edge, and top buttonhole 1" (2.5 cm) from top edge. Space other three buttonholes about 3¼ (3½, 3¾, 4, 4¼)" (8.5 [9, 9.5, 10, 11] cm) apart. To work buttonholes on right-side rows: k3, yarn over, knit 2 together, knit to end of row.

■ SLEEVES

With larger needles, cast on 28 (30, 30, 34, 34) stitches. Working in stockinette stitch, work 2" (5 cm) even ending with a wrong-side row. Increase 1 stitch each edge on next row, then every 8 rows 2 times, then every 10 rows 6 times for a total of 46 (48, 48, 52, 52) stitches. Work even to a total length of 18 (18, 19, 20, 20)" [46 (46, 48.5, 51, 51) cm]. *Shape cap:* Bind off 4 stitches at beginning of next 2 rows. Decrease 1 stitch each edge every other row 12 (12, 12, 14, 14) times. Work decreases as follows: on right-side rows, knit 1, knit 2 together, knit to last 3 stitches, ssk (see page 23), knit 1. Bind off 5 stitches at beginning of next 2 rows. Bind off remaining 4 (6, 6, 6, 6) stitches.

■ FINISHING

Using backstitch (see Basics, page 92), with right sides together, sew shoulder seams. Using mattress stitch (see Basics, page 88), from right side of work, sew side and sleeve seams, reversing seaming for 1" (2.5 cm) at bottom to allow for roll. With right sides together, set sleeve into armhole, easing to fit. Sew sleeve into armhole using backstitch.

CHOOSING BUTTONS

Choosing just the right button is a great way to individualize a cardigan. This is one detail where mass manufacturers often cut corners, but when you are creating a one-of-a-kind garment you have the luxury of splurging on a really effective button. Even when it's desirable to have the buttons blend into the sweater, quality natural materials such as shell, wood, or bone add a touch of elegance.

When you're choosing buttons, there are just a few factors to consider. The first is weight. A heavy button will eventually stretch the button side of your cardigan so that the fronts will be two different lengths when it's worn open. Stretching can be remedied in most cases by reinforcing the buttonband, usually by sewing a ribbon behind it. For a rolled-edge sweater with no formal band it is best to choose a lightweight button. The second factor to consider is shape. An oddly-shaped button requires a large buttonhole. The third factor to consider is compatibility of care. If your sweater is washable and the buttons are not, you may have to remove and replace them every time you launder your sweater. Keeping these considerations in mind, have fun choosing buttons.

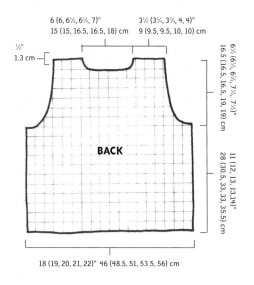

6 (6, 6½, 6½, 7)"
15 (15, 16.5, 16.5, 18) cm

3½ (3¾, 3¾, 4, 4)"
9 (9.5, 9.5, 10, 10) cm

½"
1.3 cm

BACK

6½ (6½, 6½, 7½, 7½)"
16.5 (16.5, 16.5, 19, 19) cm

11 (12, 13, 13, 14)"
28 (30.5, 33, 33, 35.5) cm

18 (19, 20, 21, 22)" 46 (48.5, 51, 53.5, 56) cm

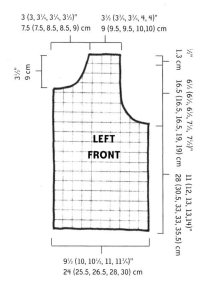

3 (3, 3¼, 3¼, 3½)"
7.5 (7.5, 8.5, 8.5, 9) cm

3½ (3¾, 3¾, 4, 4)"
9 (9.5, 9.5, 10, 10) cm

½"
1.3 cm

3½"
9 cm

LEFT FRONT

6½ (6½, 6½, 7½, 7½)"
16.5 (16.5, 16.5, 19, 19) cm

11 (12, 13, 13, 14)"
28 (30.5, 33, 33, 35.5) cm

9½ (10, 10½, 11, 11¾)"
24 (25.5, 26.5, 28, 30) cm

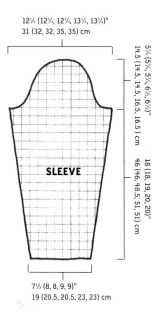

12¼ (12¾, 12¾, 13¾, 13¾)"
31 (32, 32, 35, 35) cm

5¾ (5¾, 5¾, 6½, 6½)"
14.5 (14.5, 14.5, 16.5, 16.5) cm

SLEEVE

18 (18, 19, 20, 20)"
46 (46, 48.5, 51, 51) cm

7½ (8, 8, 9, 9)"
19 (20.5, 20.5, 23, 23) cm

Mark for buttons: Using safety pins, mark positions for five buttons evenly spaced along left front edge (on 4th stitch from edge) and matching corresponding buttonholes on right front. Sew on buttons as marked. If desired, work buttonhole stitch around buttonholes. *Neck Edge:* With smaller needles and right-side facing, pick up about 68 (72, 72, 76, 76) stitches (see page 47) around neck edge, beginning and ending at center fronts. Beginning with a purl row, work in stockinette stitch for 1½" (3.8 cm). Bind off all stitches. Weave in loose ends. Sew buttons on left front as marked.

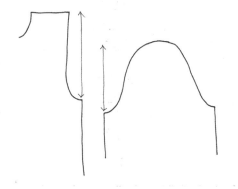

SETTING A SLEEVE INTO AN ARMHOLE

There is a certain amount of easing involved in setting a sleeve into an armhole because the sleeve cap is not exactly identical in shape to the armhole. Traditionally, a sleeve cap is 1½–2" (3.8–5 cm) shorter than the armhole depth and the curve is more dramatic than the armhole curve. Working with right sides together, match sleeve seam to side seam, pin in place, then match center top of sleeve cap to shoulder seam and pin in place. Gradually pin areas in between, easing to fit as necessary. Sew in place with backstitch (see Basics, page 92).

BUTTONHOLES

There are several methods for creating neat, professional buttonholes. For our purposes we will discuss the simplest methods. For small buttons or medium-size buttons on bulky yarn, the easiest buttonhole to create is a knit 2 together either preceded or followed by a yarnover. This buttonhole is complete in just one row (Figure 1).

Figure 3

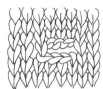

Figure 5

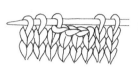

Figure 4

Figure 1
yarnover
followed by
a knit 2
together

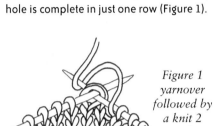

Figure 2
knit 2 together
followed by a
yarnover

On the next row the yarnover is worked as a stitch (Figure 2). For larger buttonholes, the procedure is worked over 2 rows. On the first buttonhole row, bind off the desired number of stitches, usually 2 or 3 (Figure 3). On the next row, cast on the same number of stitches over the bound-off stitches. To cast on these stitches, use the simple backwards loop method (Figure 4). Continue your knitting as established and you'll have a completed buttonhole (Figure 5). When the garment is completed, finish off your buttonholes and keep them from stretching out with wear by working around them in buttonhole stitch (Figure 6).

Note: If you are working with a bulky yarn and wish to avoid more bulk, do your buttonhole stitch in a thinner yarn in a matching color, or if you're using a plied yarn, separate the plies to make a thinner strand.

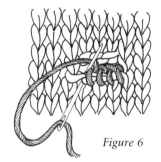

Figure 6

SEWING ON A BUTTON

If you're knitting with a plied yarn, you can sew your buttons on with one of the plies or you can use a matching sewing thread doubled. Using a blunt-end needle that will fit through the hole in the button, insert the needle from the wrong side of the knitted fabric into the button leaving about ¼" (6 mm) between the button and the knitted fabric (Figure 1). Take the needle through the next hole in the button and back into the fabric. Repeat this step as many times as you have button holes; end on the right side of the garment but under the button. To finish off, wrap your yarn or thread three to five times under the button and pull the yarn or thread through the thickness and back to the wrong side of the knitted fabric (Figure 2). Fasten off.

Figure 1

Figure 2

EVERYBODY'S
VEST

This vest is truly for everybody. Its personality can change dramatically by choice of yarn, moving its look from feminine to masculine, dressy to sporty. Choice of size can give it the look of being on the skinny-fitting fashion edge or comfortably easy fitting for grandpa. Replace the ribs with rolls and soften up the edges. Lengthen or shorten the body. A classic vest is a timeless piece of knitting.

■ SIZE	■ YARN	■ NEEDLES	■ NOTIONS	■ GAUGE
36 (40, 44, 46, 50)" (91.5 [101.5, 112, 117, 127] cm) bust/chest circumference. Vest shown measures 40" (101.5) cm.	Double-knitting (DK) or light worsted-weight yarn, about 850 (950, 1000, 1050, 1150) yd (778 [869, 915, 961, 1052] m). We used Garn Studio Karisma Angora-Tweed (30% angora, 70% lambs wool; 158 yd [145 m]/50 g): 6 (6, 7, 7, 8) balls #04, soft olive.	Body—size 7 (4.5 mm). Ribbing—size 5 (3.75 mm): straight and 16" (40-cm) circular needle for neck. Adjust needle size if necessary to obtain the correct gauge.	Tapestry needle; cable needle; row counter (optional); stitch markers.	19 stitches and 24 rows = 4" (10 cm) in box stitch; 24 stitches = 4" (10 cm) in staghorn cable on size 7 (4.5 cm) needles.

■ **STITCH GUIDE**

2 × 2 Rib (worked over a multiple of 4 + 2 stitches)
Row 1: (right side) *Purl 2, knit 2*. Repeat from * to * across row. End purl 2.
Row 2: *Knit 2, purl 2*. Repeat from * to * across row. End knit 2.
Repeat Rows 1 and 2 for pattern.

Box Stitch (worked over a total of 4 + 2 stitches and 6 rows)
Row 1 and 3: (wrong side) *Purl 2, knit 2*. Repeat from * to * across row. End purl 2.
Row 2: Work stitches as they appear.
Row 4 and 6: (right side) *Purl 2, knit 2*. Repeat from * to * across row. End purl 2.
Row 5: Work stitches as they appear.
Repeat Rows 1 through 6 for pattern.

Staghorn Cable (worked over 20 stitches and 6 rows)
Note: There are two cable twists that are used in the staghorn cable. They will be abbreviated as follows:
BC (Back Cross): Slip 2 stitches to cable needle and hold in back of work, knit 2, knit 2 from cable needle.
FC (Front Cross): Slip 2 stitches to cable needle and hold in front of work, knit 2, knit 2 from cable needle.
Row 1, 3 and 5: (wrong side of work) Knit 2, purl 16, knit 2.
Row 2: Purl 2, knit 4, BC, FC, knit 4, purl 2.
Row 4: Purl 2, knit 2, BC, knit 4, FC, knit 2, purl 2.
Row 6: Purl 2, BC, knit 8, FC, purl 2.
Repeat Rows 1 through 6 for pattern.

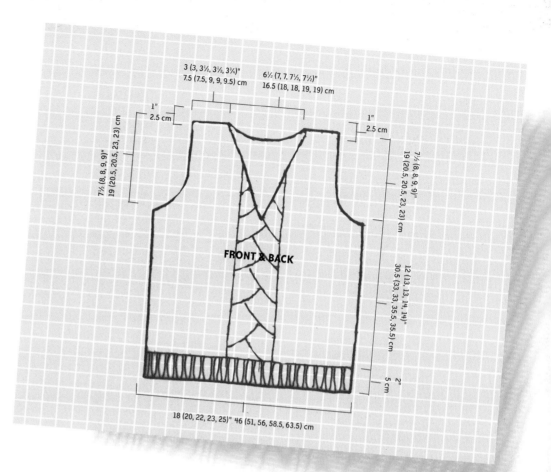

3 (3, 3½, 3½, 3¾)"
7.5 (7.5, 9, 9, 9.5) cm

6½ (7, 7, 7½, 7½)"
16.5 (18, 18, 19, 19) cm

1"
2.5 cm

1"
2.5 cm

7½ (8, 8, 9, 9)"
19 (20.5, 20.5, 23, 23) cm

7½ (8, 8, 9, 9)"
19 (20.5, 20.5, 23, 23) cm

FRONT & BACK

12 (13, 13, 14, 14)"
30.5 (33, 33, 35.5, 35.5) cm

2"
5 cm

18 (20, 22, 23, 25)" 46 (51, 56, 58.5, 63.5) cm

BACK

With ribbing needles, cast on 86 (98, 106, 110, 118) stitches. Work 2" (5 cm) in 2 × 2 rib, ending with a right-side row. Change to body needles and box stitch and work even to 14 (15, 15, 16, 16)" (35.5 [38, 38, 40.5, 40.5] cm) from cast on edge. *Shape armhole:* Bind off 5 stitches at beginning of next 2 rows. Decrease 1 stitch each edge every other row 8 (12, 15, 16, 18) times—60 (64, 66, 68, 72) stitches. Work even until armhole measures 7½ (8, 8, 9, 9)" (19 [20.5, 20.5, 23, 23] cm] ending with a wrong-side row. *Shape neck and shoulders:* Place marker either side of center 26 (28, 28, 30, 30) stitches. Bind off 5 (5, 5, 5, 6) stitches at beginning of row, work to first marker. Attach a second ball of yarn (see page 47) and bind off center 26 (28, 28, 30, 30) stitches. Remove markers and work to end of row. One shoulder has 12 (13, 14, 14, 15) stitches, the other shoulder has 17 (18, 19, 19, 21) stitches. Working each side with a separate ball of yarn, bind off 5 (5, 5, 5, 6) stitches at beginning of next row, then 3 stitches at neck edge of opposite shoulder. One shoulder has 9 (10, 11, 11, 12) stitches, the other 12 (13, 14, 14, 15) stitches. Bind off 5 (5, 5, 5, 6) stitches at beginning of next row, then 3 stitches at neck edge of opposite shoulder. One shoulder has 4 (5, 6, 6) stitches, the other has 9 (10, 11, 11, 12) stitches. Bind off 5 (5, 5, 5, 6) stitches at beginning of next row and 4 (5, 6, 6, 6) stitches at beginning of next 2 rows.

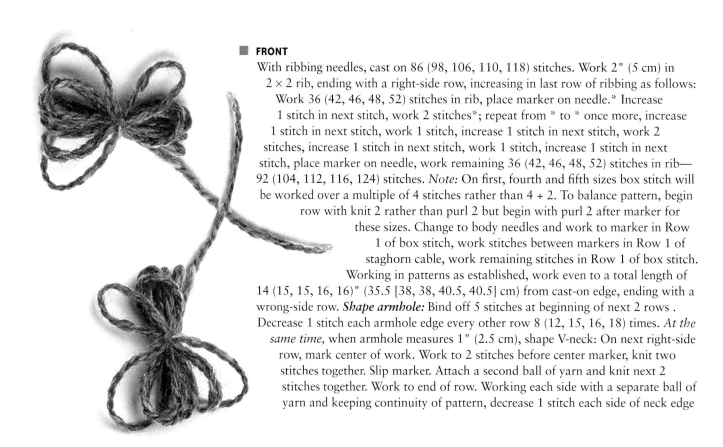

■ FRONT

With ribbing needles, cast on 86 (98, 106, 110, 118) stitches. Work 2" (5 cm) in 2 × 2 rib, ending with a right-side row, increasing in last row of ribbing as follows: Work 36 (42, 46, 48, 52) stitches in rib, place marker on needle.* Increase 1 stitch in next stitch, work 2 stitches*; repeat from * to * once more, increase 1 stitch in next stitch, work 1 stitch, increase 1 stitch in next stitch, work 2 stitches, increase 1 stitch in next stitch, work 1 stitch, increase 1 stitch in next stitch, place marker on needle, work remaining 36 (42, 46, 48, 52) stitches in rib— 92 (104, 112, 116, 124) stitches. *Note:* On first, fourth and fifth sizes box stitch will be worked over a multiple of 4 stitches rather than 4 + 2. To balance pattern, begin row with knit 2 rather than purl 2 but begin with purl 2 after marker for these sizes. Change to body needles and work to marker in Row 1 of box stitch, work stitches between markers in Row 1 of staghorn cable, work remaining stitches in Row 1 of box stitch. Working in patterns as established, work even to a total length of 14 (15, 15, 16, 16)" (35.5 [38, 38, 40.5, 40.5] cm) from cast-on edge, ending with a wrong-side row. *Shape armhole:* Bind off 5 stitches at beginning of next 2 rows . Decrease 1 stitch each armhole edge every other row 8 (12, 15, 16, 18) times. *At the same time,* when armhole measures 1" (2.5 cm), shape V-neck: On next right-side row, mark center of work. Work to 2 stitches before center marker, knit two stitches together. Slip marker. Attach a second ball of yarn and knit next 2 stitches together. Work to end of row. Working each side with a separate ball of yarn and keeping continuity of pattern, decrease 1 stitch each side of neck edge

KEEPING TRACK OF STITCH PATTERNS

Complex knitting can involve keeping concurrent track of different patterns. When you're working simultaneously on different stitch patterns, it is advisable to separate the patterns with stitch markers. Markers serve as a reminder when you're knitting along that something different is supposed to happen. They also make for easy referencing and counting of stitches.

Keeping track of rows can present a greater challenge. A row counter is an indispensable tool for easy counting. They come in several different sizes to slip on to the end of a knitting needle. Simply turn the counter for every row completed, starting over when you complete a full pattern repeat. In a perfect world, the stitch patterns will all repeat over the same number of rows. When this is the case, you can simply consult the same row in each pattern-stitch description and proceed accordingly—for example, knitting every Row 2 or 5 at the same time. In a slightly less than perfect world, there will be a simple common denominator so that three simultaneous patterns might repeat over 2, 4, and 8 rows respectively, and you can easily every other row 18 (19, 19, 20, 20) times—14 (15, 16, 16, 18) stitches remain on each shoulder. *Note:* Work cable crosses for as long as possible as number of stitches permits. When there are not enough stitches to complete cables, work remaining cable stitches as they appear on needles. When front measures same length as back to shoulders, bind off at each shoulder edge 5 stitches 2 times, then 4 stitches once for first size; 5 stitches 3 times for second size; 5 stitches 2 times, then 6 stitches once for third and fourth sizes; and 6 stitches 3 times for fifth size.

■ **FINISHING**

Backstitch (see Basics, page 92) shoulder seams. With ribbing needles, right side of work facing and beginning at armhole bind-off, pick up 106 (110, 110, 120, 120) stitches evenly around armhole (see page 47). Work 6 rows in 2 × 2 rib. Bind off all stitches. Sew side seams using backstitch. *Neck Rib:* With right side of work facing, circular needles and beginning at right shoulder, pick up 30 (34, 34, 34, 34) stitches across back neck edge, 44 (48, 48, 52, 52) stitches from left shoulder to point of V, 1 stitch at point of V, 44 (48, 48, 52, 52) stitches from point of V to right shoulder—119 (131, 131, 139, 139) stitches. Join stitches into a circle, placing marker at beginning of round. Work in 2 × 2 rib, beginning at right shoulder with knit 2, and working knit 2 before and after stitch at point of V, plus knit the V stitch. End round at right shoulder with purl 2. Keeping continuity of patterns, on next round work to 1 stitch before V stitch. Slip next 2 stitches together as if to knit, knit 1, pass slipped stitches over, work in pattern to end of round. Repeat this round 5 more times. Bind off all stitches. Weave in loose ends.

figure out working four repeats of the 2-row pattern and two repeats of the 4-row pattern for every one repeat of the 8-row pattern. Often when there are short repeats a pattern can be easily memorized. The use of a row counter or other method of record is still recommended for easy reference between knitting sessions.

Some patterns have no easy repeat or small common denominator. One pattern might repeat over 28 rows while the other repeats over 34 rows. In this case there are several ways of keeping track. Some knitters use multiple row counters, color coding them to tell which pattern is which. Others use index cards for each row of each pattern and simply flip them as they go along or create charts of columns listing each row, calculating the total number of rows per piece of a garment and plotting out the sequences. Stitch charts are also an alternative. Use a pencil and keep a tally of each row.

Find the method that works best for you. The most important thing to remember is to organize ahead of time and keep a record. As tempting as it is to jump right into a new pattern, a small amount of time spent on knitting preparation can prevent frustration while knitting.

HOODIE
SWEATSHIRT

Everybody needs at least one of these classics. Make it in a luxurious merino yarn, and it attains a new elegance but remains as comfortable as the namesake's cotton fleece. The hood requires a little more knitting, but it is well worth the extra hours for the years of wear the sweatshirt will provide.

■ SIZE	■ YARN	■ NEEDLES	■ NOTIONS	■ GAUGE
42 (44, 46, 48, 52)" (106.5 [112, 117, 122, 132] cm) bust/chest circumference. Sweater shown measures 44" (112 cm).	Worsted-weight yarn, about 1350 (1400, 1450, 1500, 1600) yd (1236 [1283,1328, 1374, 1465] m). We used Morehouse Farms Merino 3-Ply (100% merino wool; 145 yd [133 m]/2 oz [28 g]): 10 (10, 10, 11, 12) skeins, seafoam.	Ribbing—Size 6 (4 mm): straight and 24" (60-cm) circular needle for hood ribbing. Body—Size 8 (5 mm). Drawstring—Size 3 (3.25 mm), 2 double-pointed needles.	22" (56 cm) separating zipper; four 6½" (16.5 cm) stitch holders; tapestry needle; safety pins, straight pins, and sewing needle and thread for inserting zipper.	16 stitches and 24 rows = 4" (10 cm) in stockinette stitch on size 8 (5 mm) needles.

STITCH GUIDE

1 × 1 Rib (worked over an even number of stitches)
Row 1: *Knit 1, purl 1*. Repeat from * to * across row.
Repeat this row for pattern.

Stockinette Stitch
Row 1: (right side) Knit all stitches.
Row 2: Purl all stitches.
Repeat Rows 1 and 2 for pattern.

Note All sizes are the same length due to the length of separating zippers. If adjusting length make sure to find a separating zipper that matches the new front length from bottom edge to neck edge. The zipper may be up to 1" (2.5 cm) shorter than that length, but not longer.

BACK

With ribbing needles, cast on 84 (88, 92, 96, 104) stitches. Work in 1 × 1 rib until piece measures 3" (7.5 cm). Change to body needles and stockinette stitch and work even to a total length of 23" (58.5 cm) from cast-on edge. *Shape neck:* Mark center 26 (30, 30, 32, 32) stitches. Work to marker. Attach a second ball of yarn (see page 47) and bind off center 26 (30, 30, 32, 32) stitches. Work to end of row. Working each side with a separate ball of yarn, bind off each side of neck edge 3 stitches once. When work measures 24" (61 cm), place remaining 26 (26, 28, 29, 33) stitches each side on holders for shoulders.

RIGHT FRONT

With ribbing needles, cast on 42 (44, 46, 48, 52) stitches. Work in 1 × 1 rib until piece measures 3" (7.5 cm). Change to body needles and stockinette stitch and work even to a total length of 22" (56 cm) from cast-on edge, ending with a wrong-side row. *Shape neck:* Bind off 4 (6, 6, 7, 7) stitches at beginning of next row. *All sizes: At neck edge, work every other row as follows,* bind off 4 stitches 2 times, 2 stitches once, then 1 stitch 2 times. When front measures 24" (61 cm) place remaining 26 (26, 28, 29, 33) stitches on holder for shoulders.

LEFT FRONT

Work same as for right front, reversing neck shaping.

SLEEVES:

With ribbing needles, cast on 32 (36, 36, 40, 40) stitches. Work in 1 × 1 rib for 3" (7.5 cm), increasing 4 stitches evenly across last row—36 (40, 40, 44, 44) stitches. Change to body needles and stockinette stitch. Increase 1 stitch each edge every 4 rows 9 times, then every 6 rows 9 times—

72 (76, 76,80, 80) stitches. When sleeve measures 18 (18, 18, 19, 19)" (46 [46, 46, 48.5, 48.5] cm) for women or 19 (20, 20, 21, 21)" (48.5 [51, 51, 53.5, 53.5] cm) for men from cast-on edge, bind off all stitches.

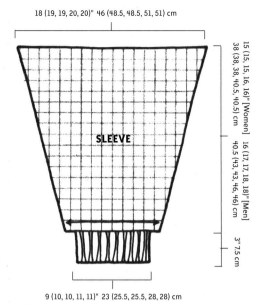

18 (19, 19, 20, 20)" 46 (48.5, 48.5, 51, 51) cm

15 (15, 15, 16)"[Women] 38 (38, 38, 40.5, 40.5] cm

16 (17, 17, 18, 18)"[Men] 40.5 (43, 43, 46, 46] cm

3" 7.5 cm

SLEEVE

9 (10, 10, 11, 11)" 23 (25.5, 25.5, 28, 28) cm

◼ POCKET

With body needles, cast on 32 stitches. Work 3" (7.5 cm) even ending with a wrong-side row. Decrease 1 stitch at beginning of next row and at same edge every other row 11 more times. When work measures 7" (18 cm) bind off remaining 20 stitches. Make another pocket reversing shaping. *Pocket Rib:* With ribbing needles, pick up 24 stitches evenly along diagonal edge of pocket. Work ½" (1.3 cm) in 1 × 1 rib. Bind off.

◼ HOOD

With body needles, cast on 38 (40, 40, 42, 42) stitches. Work even in stockinette stitch until work measures 10" (25.5 cm). Decrease 1 stitch at beginning of next row and at the same edge every 4 rows 5 more times. When work measures 14" (35.5 cm) bind off remaining 32 (34, 34, 36, 36) stitches. Make another side reversing all shaping.

◼ DRAWSTRING

With double-pointed needles, cast on 3 stitches. Work I-cord (see page 19) for a total length of 45" (114.5 cm). Bind off stitches leaving 4" (10 cm) tail. With threaded tapestry needle, bring yarn tail through center of I-cord to secure.

◼ FINISHING

Using backstitch (see Basics, page 92), sew hood pieces together along top and shaped edge. With circular needle, pick up (see page 47) 120 stitches evenly along straight edge of hood. Work 1¾" (4.5 cm) in 1 × 1 rib. Bind off. Fold rib in half to wrong side of work and slipstitch (see Basics, page 93) bound off edge to hood, keeping bottom edges open. Knit shoulders together (see page 54). Mark center top of sleeve and mark front and back 9 (9½, 9½, 10, 10)" (23 [24, 24, 25.5, 25.5] cm) down from shoulder seam. Pin sleeve to body, matching center top of sleeve to shoulder seam and edges of sleeve to markers on body. Backstitch (see Basics, page 92) sleeve to body. Sew side and sleeve seams using mattress stitch (see Basics, page 92). Pin pockets to fronts placing bottom edge of pockets even with top of ribbing and straight-side edge of pockets even with second stitch from front edge. Slipstitch in place along all unribbed edges, leaving ribbed edge open. *Inserting zipper:* Pin zipper to front edges, having edges meet at center of zipper, placing bottom edge of zipper even with bottom edge of sweater and top of zipper-pull even with top edge of sweater. Fold extra length of zipper tape forward so that it is hidden between zipper and sweater. With coordinating thread and using a backstitch, sew zipper in place keeping stitches ½" (1.3 cm) from zipper teeth. Whipstitch edges of zipper to wrong side of knitted fabric. *Attaching hood:* Using safety pins, pin bottom edge of hood to neck edge butting edges and easing neck edge to fit. With right side of work facing, slipstitch hood to neck edge. *Note:* Check inside edge after hood is stitched in place; if raw edges are showing, slipstitch those as well. Thread drawstring through hood rib. Weave in all loose ends.

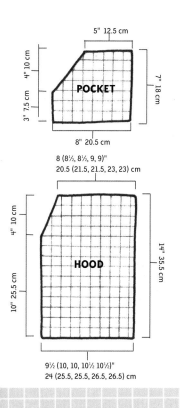

POCKET

5" 12.5 cm
4" 10 cm
7" 18 cm
3" 7.5 cm
8" 20.5 cm

HOOD

8 (8½, 8½, 9, 9)"
20.5 (21.5, 21.5, 23, 23) cm
4" 10 cm
14" 35.5 cm
10" 25.5 cm
9½ (10, 10, 10½ 10½)"
24 (25.5, 25.5, 26.5, 26.5) cm

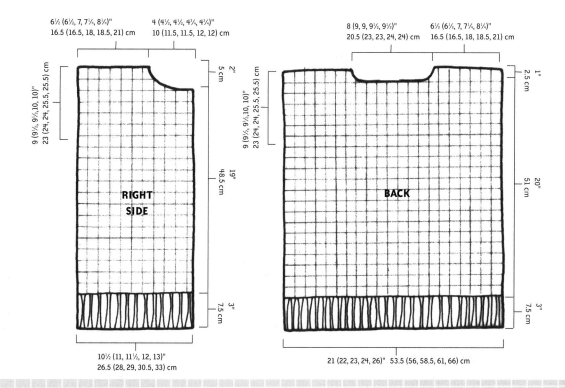

RIGHT SIDE

6½ (6½, 7, 7¼, 8¼)"
16.5 (16.5, 18, 18.5, 21) cm
4 (4½, 4½, 4¾, 4¾)"
10 (11.5, 11.5, 12, 12) cm
2"
5 cm
9 (9½, 9½, 10, 10)"
23 (24, 24, 25.5, 25.5) cm
19"
48.5 cm
3"
7.5 cm
10½ (11, 11½, 12, 13)"
26.5 (28, 29, 30.5, 33) cm

BACK

8 (9, 9, 9½, 9½)"
20.5 (23, 23, 24, 24) cm
6½ (6½, 7, 7¼, 8¼)"
16.5 (16.5, 18, 18.5, 21) cm
1"
2.5 cm
9 (9½, 9½, 10, 10)"
23 (24, 24, 25.5, 25.5) cm
20"
51 cm
3"
7.5 cm
21 (22, 23, 24, 26)" 53.5 (56, 58.5, 61, 66) cm

INSERTING A ZIPPER

Zippers in knitted garments are best inserted by hand with a sewing needle and thread because the knitted fabric is generally too bulky and stretchy to be stitched on a sewing machine. If you plan on zipping up that knit, plan ahead. The edge where the zipper is to be inserted needs to be stabilized in the knitting process either by slipping the edge stitch on the right side of the work or working a ribbing. It may be preferable to work a row of slipstitch crochet along the opening edge.

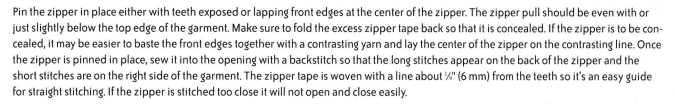

Whether the zipper is installed with the teeth exposed or concealed is a matter of preference relating to the style of the garment. In a very sporty garment the zipper may become a design element to be played up. At the edge of a cushion where a zipper is inserted for practical reasons, it is generally preferable to keep it concealed. Also, it is not always possible to get a perfect color match in a zipper and that may be another reason to conceal it.

Zipper length is easy to adjust in a non-separating zipper. If the zipper is too long, simply sew across the teeth securely at the desired length, either with heavy-duty thread or machine stitching, and cut off the remainder. Separating zippers, however, are not as easy to adjust. They can sometimes be cut professionally, but, if that service is not available to you, be sure to adjust your garment length according to the zipper length. The zipper should be the same length or up to one inch (2.5 cm) shorter than the front length from bottom edge to neck opening. A zipper that is too long for its opening will stretch the opening longer than the rest of the garment or cause it to ripple.

Pin the zipper in place either with teeth exposed or lapping front edges at the center of the zipper. The zipper pull should be even with or just slightly below the top edge of the garment. Make sure to fold the excess zipper tape back so that it is concealed. If the zipper is to be concealed, it may be easier to baste the front edges together with a contrasting yarn and lay the center of the zipper on the contrasting line. Once the zipper is pinned in place, sew it into the opening with a backstitch so that the long stitches appear on the back of the zipper and the short stitches are on the right side of the garment. The zipper tape is woven with a line about ¼" (6 mm) from the teeth so it's an easy guide for straight stitching. If the zipper is stitched too close it will not open and close easily.

BOYFRIEND
SWEATER

Of course you'll knit a sweater for him, but face it, you'll covet it the whole time. So go ahead and make it, then borrow it—it'll probably become yours anyway. Better yet, teach him to knit!

◼ SIZE

40 (43, 46, 49, 52)" (101.5 [109, 117, 124.5, 132] cm) bust/chest circumference. Sizes are unisex. If you like an oversized sweater, choose a size that's at least 6" (15 cm) larger than your bust/chest circumference. Sweater shown measures 43" (109) cm. *Note: For women's version make sleeves 2" (5 cm) shorter than for men.*

◼ YARN

Worsted-weight yarn, about 1100 (1150, 1200, 1250, 1350) yd (1006 (1052, 1098, 1143, 1235] m) color A for both pullover and cardigan versions; about 120 (125, 130, 140, 150) yd (110 [115, 119, 128, 137] m) color B for pullover version; about 150 (160, 175, 185, 200) yd (138 [147, 160, 170, 183] m) color B for cardigan version.

We used Classic Elite Waterspun (felted, 100% merino wool; 138 yd [123 m]/50 g): 9 (9, 10, 10, 11) balls color #5093 electric blue (A) for both pullover and cardigan versions and 1 (1, 1, 2, 2) balls color #5075 grey (B) for pullover version, 2 (2, 2, 2, 2) balls gray (B) for cardigan version.

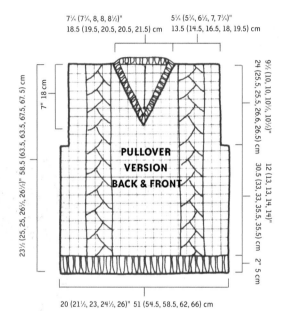

7¼ (7¾, 8, 8, 8½)" 18.5 (19.5, 20.5, 20.5, 21.5) cm

5¼ (5¾, 6½, 7, 7¾)" 13.5 (14.5, 16.5, 18, 19.5) cm

9½ (10, 10, 10½, 10½)" 24 (25.5, 25.5, 26.6, 26.5) cm

7" 18 cm

23½ (25, 25, 26½, 26½)" 58.5 (63.5, 63.5, 67.5, 67.5) cm

12 (13, 13, 14, 14)" 30.5 (33, 33, 35.5, 35.5) cm

2" 5 cm

PULLOVER VERSION BACK & FRONT

20 (21½, 23, 24½, 26)" 51 (54.5, 58.5, 62, 66) cm

19 (20, 20, 21, 21)" 48.5 (51, 51, 53.5, 53.5) cm

21 (22, 22, 23, 23)" 53.5 (56, 56, 58.5, 58.5) cm

SLEEVES

19 (20, 20, 21, 21)" 48.5 (51, 51, 53.5, 53.5) cm

2" 5 cm

9 (9¾, 9¾, 9¾, 10½)" 23 (25, 25, 25, 26.5) cm

◼ STITCH GUIDE

1 × 1 Rib (worked over an even number of stitches)
Row 1: *Knit 1, purl 1*. Repeat from * to * across row. Repeat this row for pattern.

1 × 1 Rib (worked over an odd number of stitches)
Row 1: *Knit 1, purl 1*; repeat from * to *, end row knit 1.
Row 2: *Purl 1, knit 1*; repeat from * to *, end row purl 1.
Repeat Rows 1 and 2 for pattern.

6 × 1 Rib (worked over a multiple of 7 stitches + 6)
Row 1: Knit 6, *purl 1, knit 6*. Repeat from * to * across row.
Row 2: Purl 6, *knit 1, purl 6*. Repeat from * to * across row.
Repeat Rows 1 and 2 for pattern.

15-Stitch Front/Back Cross Cable (worked over a panel of 15 stitches)
Row 1, 3, 7 and 9: (right side) Purl 1, knit 6, purl 1, knit 6, purl 1.
Row 2 and all even-numbered rows: Knit 1, purl 6, knit 1, purl 6, knit 1.
Row 5: Purl 1, slip next 3 stitches to cable needle and hold in front of work, knit 3, knit 3 stitches from cable needle, purl 1, slip next 3 stitches to cable needle and hold in back of work, knit 3, knit 3 stitches from cable needle, purl 1.
Row 10: Work as Row 2.
Repeat Rows 1–10 for pattern.

Size 6, 7 and 8 (4, 4.5 and 5 mm): straight. Size 6 (4 mm): 24" (60-cm) circular for neck (pullover version) and 29" (80-cm) or longer circular needle (cardigan version). Adjust needle size if necessary to obtain the correct gauge.

Cable needle; stitch markers; row counter; four stitch holders about 6" (15 cm) long; four stitch holders about 4½" (11.5 cm) long for cardigan version; (optional) seven ¾" (2 cm) buttons for cardigan version.

18 stitches and 26 rows = 4" (10 cm) in stockinette stitch on size 8 (5 mm) needles.

PULLOVER VERSION

■ **BACK**

With B and size 7 (4.5 mm) needles, cast on 90 (97, 104, 111, 118) stitches. Work in 1 × 1 rib for 2" (5 cm) ending with a right-side row. Purl 1 row. Change to A, size 8 (5 mm) needles, and set up pattern as follows: work 13 stitches in Row 1 of 6 × 1 rib, place marker, work next 15 stitches in Row 1 of cable, place marker, work 34 (41, 48, 55, 62) stitches in Row 1 of 6 × 1 rib, place marker, work next 15 stitches in Row 1 of cable pattern, place marker, work 13 stitches in Row 1 of 6 × 1 Rib. Work even in patterns as established to a total length of 14 (15, 15, 16, 16)" (35.5 [38, 38, 40.5, 40.5] cm) from cast on. *Shape armhole:* Bind off 5 stitches at beginning of next 2 rows. Keeping continuity of pattern, work even on 80 (87, 94, 101, 108) stitches until armhole measures 9½ (10, 10, 10½, 10½)" (24 [25.5, 25.5, 26.5, 26.5] cm), ending with a wrong-side row. On next row, remove markers as you work across 24 (26, 29, 32, 35) stitches and place on holder. Bind off next 32 (35, 36, 37, 38) stitches for back of neck, work across remaining 24 (26, 29, 32, 35) stitches and place on second holder. Cut yarn.

■ **FRONT**

Work same as for back until armhole measures 2½ (3, 3, 3½, 3½)" (6.5 [7.5, 7.5, 9, 9] cm), ending with a wrong-side row. *Shape neck, decrease row:* Mark center of work. *For first, third and fifth sizes:* Work in pattern as established to 3 stitches before center. Knit 2 together, knit 1. Attach a second ball of yarn. Knit 1, ssk (see page 23), work in pattern to end of row. *For second and fourth sizes:* Mark center stitch. Work in patterns as established to 3 stitches before center stitch. Knit 2 together, knit 1. Attach a second ball of yarn and bind off center stitch. With 1 stitch on needle from bind off, work ssk using next 2 stitches, work in pattern to end of row. *All sizes:* Working each side separately (see page 47) and keeping continuity of patterns, repeat decrease row (do not bind off any more center stitches) every other row 10 (11, 14, 14, 16) more times, then every 4 rows 5 (5, 3, 3, 3) times. When front measures same length as back, place remaining shoulder stitches on stitch holders. Each shoulder will have 24 (26, 29, 32, 35) stitches.

SLEEVES

With B and size 6 (4 mm) needles, cast on 40 (44, 44, 44, 48) stitches. Work 2" (5 cm) in 1 × 1 rib, ending with a right-side row. Purl 1 row, increasing 1 (4, 4, 4, 7) stitches evenly across row—41 (48, 48, 48, 55) stitches. Change to A and size 8 (5 mm) needles. Work in 6 × 1 rib and begin sleeve shaping as follows: maintaining increased stitches in pattern, increase 1 stitch each edge on the 3 (5, 5, 5, 5) rows, then every 4 rows 21 (20, 20, 22, 19) times—85 (90, 90, 94, 95) stitches. Work even until sleeve measures 21 (22, 22, 23, 23)" (53.5 [56, 56, 58.5, 58.5] cm) from cast-on edge for men's sizes. For women, follow sleeve instructions as presented until sleeve length is 2" (5 cm) shorter. Bind off all stitches.

FINISHING

Knit shoulder seams together (see page 54). Mark center top of sleeve. Pin sleeve to body, matching center top of sleeve to shoulder seam and edges of sleeve to armhole. Backstitch (see Basics, page 92) tops of sleeves into armholes. Remove markers. Using mattress stitch (see Basics, page 92), sew side and sleeve seams. *Neck:* With B and size 6 (4 mm) circular needles, beginning at point of V, pick up (see page 47) 37 stitches along side of V, 35 (38, 39, 40, 41) stitches across back of neck, and 37 stitches along side of V—109 (112, 113, 114, 115) stitches. Working back and forth in rows, ending and beginning at point of V, work 1¼" (3.2 cm) in 1 × 1 Rib. Bind off all stitches. Overlap rib at point of V and using threaded tapestry needle, slip-stitch into place. Weave in loose ends.

READING A CABLE CHART

Instructions for working cables are presented two ways. The first way is to spell out each row stitch by stitch, as shown below in OXOX Cable instructions, and Trellis with Moss Stitch Cable. The second way is to chart each row, indicating stitches and cable crosses with symbols. Spelling out each row is fine for simple cables. However, as cables become more complex, descriptive wording can become difficult to follow. Once you learn to read the symbols, a charted cable pattern is easier to follow and presents a clearer picture of how the finished cable will appear.

In reading a cable chart remember that right-side rows are read from right to left and wrong-side rows are read from left to right. When working wrong-side rows, it's important to remember that the chart displays the stitches as they appear on the right side of the work. For instance, on wrong-side rows, if the chart indicates a knit stitch, the knitter will purl that stitch in order for it to appear as a knit stitch on the right side of the work. In circular knitting, all chart rows are read from right to left because you are always working from the right side.

OXOX Cable - Panel of 12 stitches and 16 rows.

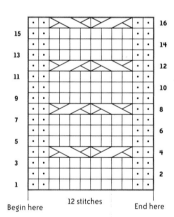

Although most charts begin on the right side, this cable pattern begins on the left side with a wrong-side row.

☐ Knit on right side; purl on wrong side

· Purl on right side; knit on wrong side

☐ Pattern repeat box

2/2 Back Cross - Place 2 stitches onto cable needle and hold in back, k2, k2 from cable needle.

2/2 Front Cross - Place 2 stitches onto cable needle and hold in front, k2, k2 from cable needle.

Rows 1 and 3: (Wrong side of work) - Knit 2, purl 8, knit 2.

Row 2: Purl 2, knit 8, purl 2.

Row 4: Purl 2, slip next 2 stitches to cable needle and hold in back of work, knit 2, then knit 2 from cable needle; slip next 2 stitches to cable needle and hold in front, knit 2, then knit 2 from cable needle; purl 2.

Rows 5, 6, and 7: Repeat Rows 1, 2, and 3.

Row 8: Purl 2, slip next 2 stitches to cable needle and hold in front, knit 2, then knit 2 from cable needle; slip next 2 stitches to cable needle and hold in back, knit 2, then knit 2 from cable needle; purl 2.

Rows 9, 10, 11, and 12: Repeat Rows 5, 6, 7, and 8.

Rows 13, 14, 15, and 16: Repeat Rows 1, 2, 3, and 4.

Repeat Rows 1–16 for pattern.

Trellis with Moss Stitch-Panel of 28 stitches and 24 rows.

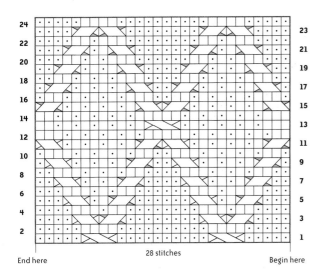

24 23
22 21
20 19
18 17
16 15
14 13
12 11
10 9
8   7
6   5
4   3
2   1

End here   28 stitches   Begin here

☐ Knit on right side; purl on wrong side

· Purl on right side; knit on wrong side

☐ Pattern repeat box

⬛ Front Double Knit Cross -Slip next 2 stitches to cable needle and hold in front, knit 2 stitches, then knit 2 stitches from cable needle.

⬛ Back Cross - Slip next stitch to cable needle and hold in back, knit 2 stitches, then purl stitch from cable needle.

⬛ Front Cross - Slip next 2 stitches to cable needle and hold in front, k1, then knit 2 stitches from cable needle.

⬛ Front Purl Cross - Slip 2 stitches to cable needle and hold in front, purl 1, then knit 2 stitches from cable needle.

SPECIAL ABBREVIATIONS

Front Double Knit Cross (FDKC) - Slip next 2 stitches to cable needle and hold in front , knit 2 stitches, then knit 2 stitches from cable needle.

Back Cross (BC) - Slip next stitch to cable needle and hold in back, knit 2 stitches, then purl stitch from cable needle.

Front Cross (FC) - Slip next 2 stitches to cable needle and hold in front, k1, then knit 2 stitches from cable needle.

Front Purl Cross (FPC) - Slip 2 stitches to cable needle and hold in front, purl 1, then knit 2 stitches from cable needle.

Row 1: (Right side of work) - Purl 5, FDKC (see special abbreviation above), purl 10, FDKC, purl 5.

Row 2 and all other wrong-side rows: Knit all knit stitches and purl all purl stitches as facing.

Row 3: Purl 4, BC (see special abbreviation above), FC (see special abbreviation above), purl 8, BC, FC, purl 4.

Row 5: Purl 3, *BC, knit 1, purl 1, FC*, purl 6, repeat from * to*, purl 3.

Row 7: Purl 2, *BC, (knit 1, purl 1) twice, FC*, purl 4, repeat from * to *, purl 2.

Row 9: Purl 1, *BC, (knit 1, purl 1) 3 times, FC*, purl 2, repeat from * to *, purl 1.

Row 11: *BC, (knit 1, purl 1) 4 times, FC; repeat from *.

Row 13: Knit 2, (knit 1, purl 1) 5 times, FDKC, (knit 1, purl 1) 5 times, knit 2.

Row 15: *FPC (see special abbreviation above); (knit 1, purl 1) 4 times, BC; repeat from *.

Row 17: Purl 1, *FPC, (knit 1, purl 1) 3 times, BC*, purl 2, repeat from * to *, purl 1.

Row 19: Purl 2, *FPC, (knit 1, purl 1) twice, BC*, purl 4, rep from * to *, purl 2.

Row 21: Purl 3, *FPC, knit 1, purl 1, BC*, purl 6, repeat from * to *, purl 3.

Row 23: Purl 4, FPC, BC, purl 8, FPC, BC, purl 4.

Row 24: Repeat Row 2.

Repeat Rows 1–24 for pattern.

Trellis with Moss Stitch

OXOX cable

CARDIGAN VERSION (sweater not shown)

■ **BACK**

Work as for pullover version.

■ **POCKET LININGS**

With A and size 8 (5 mm) needles, cast on 21 stitches. Work even in stockinette stitch to a total length of 4" (10 cm). Cut yarn and place stitches on holder. Make another to match.

■ **LEFT FRONT**

With B and size 7 (4.5 mm) needles, cast on 45 (49, 52, 56, 59) stitches. Work 2" (5 cm) in 1 × 1 rib, ending with a right-side row. Purl 1 row. Change to A and size 8 (5 mm) needles and set up pattern as follows: Work 13 stitches in Row 1 of 6 × 1 rib, place marker on needle, work next 15 stitches in Row 1 of cable pattern, place marker, work remaining 17 (21, 24, 28, 31) stitches in Row 1 of 6 × 1 rib. Work even in patterns as established to a total length of 7" (18 cm), ending with a wrong-side row. *Place pocket:* Work across 10 stitches, place next 21 stitches on holder. With right side facing, place 21 pocket stitches from one holder onto left needle and work across in pattern stitches as established on front. Work to end of row. *Note: Do not place pocket on cable twist row.* Work even to a total length of 14 (15, 15, 16, 16)" (35.5 [38, 38, 40.5, 40.5] cm) ending with a wrong-side row. *Shape armhole:* Bind off 5 stitches at beginning of next row. Keeping continuity of pattern, work even on 40 (44, 47, 51, 54) stitches until armhole measures 2½ (3, 3, 3 ½, 3½)" (6.5 [7.5, 7.5, 9, 9] cm) ending with a wrong-side row. *Shape neck, decrease row:* Work in patterns as established to last 3 stitches, knit 2 together, knit 1. Repeat decrease row every other row 10 (12, 14, 15, 15) more times, then every 4 rows 5 (5, 3, 3, 3,) times. When front measures same length as back, place remaining 24 (26, 29, 32, 35) on holder for shoulder. Remove all remaining markers and cut yarn.

■ **RIGHT FRONT**

With B and size 7 (4.5 mm) needles, cast on 45 (49, 52, 56, 59) stitches. Work 2" (5 cm) in 1 × 1 rib, ending with a right-side row. Purl 1 row. Change to A and size 8 (5 mm) needles and set up pattern as follows: Knit 3 (0, 3, 0, 3), purl 1 (1, 1, 1, 1), work next 13 (20, 20, 27, 27) stitches in 6 × 1 rib, place marker, work next 15 stitches in cable pattern, place marker,

5¼ (5¾, 6½, 7, 7¾)"
13.5 (14.5, 16.5, 18, 19.5) cm

3½ (3¾, 4, 4, 4¼)"
9 (9.5, 10, 10, 11) cm

9½ (10, 10, 10¼, 10½)"
24 (25.5, 25.5, 26.6, 26.5) cm

12 (13, 13, 14, 14)"
30.5 (33, 33, 35.5, 35.5) cm

2" 5 cm

CARDIGAN VERSION RIGHT FRONT

7" 18 cm

16½ (18, 18, 19½, 19½)" 42 (46, 46, 49.5, 49.5) cm

7" 18 cm

10 (10¾, 11½, 12½, 13)"
25.5 (26.5, 29, 31.5, 33) cm

work next 13 stitches in 6 × 1 rib. Work even in patterns as established to a total length of 7" (18 cm) ending with a wrong-side row. *Place pocket:* Work across 14 (18, 21, 25, 28) stitches in patterns as established. Place next 21 stitches on holder. Place 21 pocket stitches on left-hand needle and work across in patterns as established on front. Work across remaining 10 stitches. Work even to a total length of 14 (15, 15, 16, 16)" (35.5 [38, 38, 40.5, 40.5] cm) from cast on, ending with a right-side row. *Shape armhole:* Bind off 5 stitches at beginning of next row. Keeping continuity of patterns, work even on 40 (44, 47, 51, 54) stitches until armhole measures 2½ (3, 3, 3½, 3½)" (6.5 [7.5, 7.5, 9, 9] cm) ending with a wrong-side row. *Shape neck, decrease row:* Knit 1, ssk, work in patterns as established to end of row. Removing markers when necessary, repeat decrease row every other row 10 (12, 14, 15, 15) more times, then every 4 rows 5 (5, 3, 3, 3) times. When front measures same length as back, place remaining 24 (26, 29, 32, 35) stitches on holder for shoulder. Cut yarn.

- ### SLEEVES
Work as for pullover.

- ### FINISHING
Work as for pullover through sewing of side and sleeve seams. *Front and Neckband:* With contrasting yarn scraps, mark point of V on both fronts. With right side of work facing, color B, and 29" (80-cm) size 6 (4 mm) circular needle, pick up (see page 47) 76 (80, 80, 84, 84) stitches starting at bottom edge and working to marker, pick up 37 stitches from marker to shoulder seam, 35 (38, 39, 40, 41) stitches across back neck, 37 from shoulder seam to marker and another 76 (80, 80, 84, 84) stitches along left front edge for a total of 261 (272, 273, 282, 283) stitches. Work 1¼" (3.2 cm) in 1 × 1 rib, working seven buttonholes (see page 61) evenly spaced on left front band (right front band for women's sweater) placing lowest buttonhole ½" (1.3 cm) from bottom edge and top buttonhole even with marker on fourth row. Sew buttons on right front band (left band for women) opposite buttonholes. *Pocket ribs:* Place stitches from holder onto size 7 (4.5 mm) needle. With B, work in 1 × 1 rib for 1" (2.5 cm). Bind off all sts. Slipstitch (see Basics, page 93) pocket linings in place on backside of front, taking care not to allow stitches to show through on right side of work. With tapestry needle, weave in loose ends to wrong side of work and secure.

DREAMY
TURTLENECK

Body-conscious shaping, a close fit, and bracelet-length sleeves make this feminine classic slightly retro yet very current. It's as reminiscent of 1950s movie star glamour as it is 21st-century sleek.

■ SIZE

34 (36, 40, 42, 44)" (86.5 [91.5, 101.5, 106.5, 112] cm) bust/chest circumference. Sweater shown measures 36" (91.5 cm).

■ YARN

Worsted-weight yarn, about 700 (800, 900, 950, 1050) yd (641 [733, 825, 870, 962] m).
We used K1C2 Meringue (60% merino wool, 25% viscose, 15% polyamide; 100 yd [91 m]/50 g): 7 (8, 9, 10, 11) balls #250 geranium red.

■ NEEDLES

Body—Size 7 (4.5mm). Ribbing—Size 5 (3.75mm): straight and 16" (40-cm) circular needle for turtleneck. Adjust needle size if necessary to obtain the correct gauge.

■ NOTIONS

Tapestry needle; safety pins or T-pins for securing seams in place.

■ GAUGE

17 stitches and 24 rows = 4" in stockinette stitch on size 7 (4.5 mm) needles.

■ STITCH GUIDE

1 × 1 Rib (worked over an even number of stitches)
Row 1: *Knit 1, purl 1*. Repeat from * to * across row.
Repeat this row for pattern.

Stockinette Stitch
Row 1: (right side) Knit all stitches.
Row 2: Purl all stitches.
Repeat Rows 1 and 2 for pattern.

■ BACK

With ribbing needles, cast on 72 (76, 84, 90, 94) stitches. Work 1" (2.5 cm) in 1 × 1 rib. Change to body needles and stockinette stitch and work 1" (2.5 cm) even ending with a wrong-side row. Decrease 1 stitch each end on next row and every 6 rows 3 (3, 3, 4, 4) more times—64 (68, 76, 80, 84) stitches. Work even to 8½ (9, 9, 9½, 9½)" (21.5 [23, 23, 24, 24] cm) from cast-on edge, ending with a wrong-side row. Increase 1 stitch each edge on next row and every 6 rows 3 (3, 3, 4, 4) times more—72 (76, 84, 90, 94) stitches. Work even until stockinette-stitch section measures a total length of 13½, (14, 14, 14½, 14½)" (34.5 [35.5, 35.5 37, 37] cm) ending with a wrong-side row. *Shape armhole:* Bind off 4 stitches at beginning of next 2 rows. Decrease 1 stitch each edge every other row 5 (6, 10, 12, 14) times. Work even on 54 (56, 56, 58, 58) stitches until piece measures 5½ (6, 6, 6½, 6½)" (14 [15, 15, 16.5, 16.5] cm) above armhole shaping ending with a wrong-side row. *Shape neck and shoulders:* Knit 16 stitches. Attach a second ball of yarn (see page 47) and bind off center 22 (24, 24, 26, 26) stitches. Knit remaining 16 stitches. Working each side with a separate ball of yarn, bind off at each side of neck edge 2 stitches once, then 1 stitch once. *At the same time,* when work measures 6½ (7, 7, 7½, 7½)" (16.5 [18, 18, 19, 19] cm) above armhole shaping, *shape shoulders:* Bind off at each shoulder edge 4 stitches 2 times, then 5 stitches once.

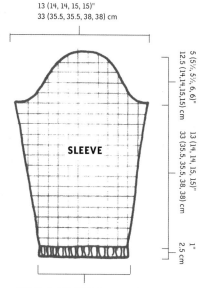

13 (14, 14, 15, 15)"
33 (35.5, 35.5, 38, 38) cm

5 (5½, 5½, 6, 6)"
12.5 (14,14,15,15) cm

13 (14, 14, 15, 15)"
33 (35.5, 35.5, 38, 38) cm

SLEEVE

1"
2.5 cm

9 (10, 10, 11, 11)" 23 (25.5, 25.5, 28, 28) cm

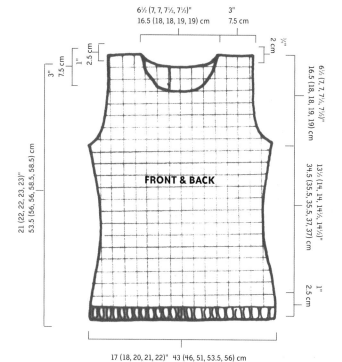

6½ (7, 7, 7½, 7½)"
16.5 (18, 18, 19, 19) cm

3"
7.5 cm

3"
7.5 cm

1"
2.5 cm

½"
2 cm

6½ (7, 7½, 7½, 7½)"
16.5 (18, 18, 19, 19) cm

FRONT & BACK

21 (22, 22, 23, 23)"
53.5 (56, 56, 58.5, 58.5) cm

13½ (14, 14, 14½, 14½)"
34.5 (35.5, 35.5, 37, 37) cm

1"
2.5 cm

17 (18, 20, 21, 22)" 43 (46, 51, 53.5, 56) cm

■ FRONT

Work same as for back until piece measures 3½ (4, 4, 4½, 4½)" (9 [10, 10, 11.5, 11.5] cm) above armhole ending with a wrong-side row. *Shape neck and shoulders:* Knit 23 stitches. Attach a second ball of yarn and bind off center 8 (10, 10, 12, 12) stitches, knit to end of row—23 stitches remain on each side of neck. Working each side of neck separately, bind off at each side of neck edge for all sizes 3 stitches once, 2 stitches 2 times, then 1 stitch 3 times. *At the same time,* when front measures same length as back to shoulders, bind off at each shoulder edge for all sizes 4 stitches 2 times, then 5 stitches once.

■ SLEEVES

With ribbing needles, cast on 38 (42, 42, 46, 46) stitches. Work 1" (2.5 cm) in 1 × 1 rib, increasing 1 stitch each edge on last row for a total of 40 (44, 44, 48, 48) stitches. Change to body needles and stockinette stitch increasing 1 stitch each edge on the 9th row of stockinette stitch, then every 8 rows 7 times—56 (60, 60, 64, 64) stitches. Work even until sleeve measures 14 (15, 15, 16, 16)" (35.5 [38, 38, 40.5, 40.5] cm) from cast-on edge, ending with a wrong-side row. *Shape cap:* Bind off 4 stitches at beginning of next 2 rows. Decrease 1 stitch each edge every right-side row 12 (14, 14, 15, 15) times, then decrease 1 stitch each edge of next 2 rows. Work remaining 20 (20, 20, 22, 22) stitches as follows: bind off 7 (7, 7, 8, 8) stitches at beginning of next 2 rows. Bind off remaining 6 stitches. Sleeve cap should measure 5 (5½, 5½, 6, 6)" (12.5 [14, 14, 15, 15] cm).

■ FINISHING

Sew shoulder seams together using backstitch (see Basics, page 92). Sew side seams using mattress stitch (see Basics, page 92). Sew sleeve seams using mattress stitch. Set sleeves into armholes with right sides together, matching sleeve seam to side seam and center top of sleeve to shoulder seam (see page 60). Ease sleeve into armhole and sew in place using backstitch. *Turtleneck:* With circular needles and right side of work facing, beginning at shoulder seam pick up 64 (66, 66, 70, 70) stitches (see page 47) evenly around neck edge. Work in 1 × 1 rib for 6 (6½, 6½, 7, 7)" (15 [16.5, 16.5, 18, 18] cm). Bind off with larger needle. With tapestry needle, weave in loose ends to wrong side of work and secure.

SHAPING

Knitted fabric is elastic by nature and therefore stretches and drapes to fit the body. A fabric knitted in a rib stitch is more elastic than stockinette and will follow the body more closely. When you desire a close fit, it can be enhanced by shaping the pieces to follow the body. In general, decreases on the body of a sweater are placed so that the front and back curve in gradually at the waist and back out at the bust and are placed vertically about one inch (2.5 cm) apart with a longer straight area at the waistline.

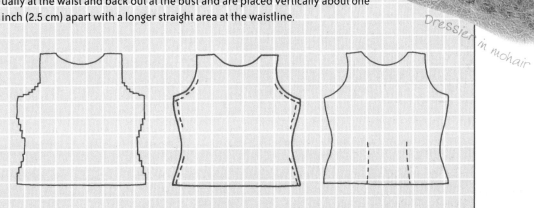

Dressier in mohair

Decreases can be incorporated in a variety of ways. The simplest is to decrease at the edge. This method is fine for a textured yarn where decreases are not visible. In a smoother yarn, and especially where the pattern does not incorporate complex stitch work, decreases and increases can become a design element or design detail. Achieve details by moving the increase or decrease in from the edge stitch to the second or third stitch from each edge and using alternate directed methods—for example, decrease by using an "ssk" at right-hand edge and a knit 2 together at left-hand edge. An advantage to this technique, besides a decorative element, is that the edges will be smooth and allow for easy seaming (as opposed to stitching the jagged edge into the seam allowance). Many knitters work increases and decreases in this manner as a matter of course just for neatness and the seaming advantage. Body shaping can also be placed further within a back or front, generally giving the effect of darts or a "princess" seam while once again allowing the outer edge to become curved but smooth.

This would be so comfy in chenille

STEPPING OUT
COAT

Your needles will fly using a super chunky yarn for this coat. The basic silhouette makes it easy to change the style from traditional to dramatic just by using a different textured yarn or varying the length. The sizing gives a slim-fitting look. If you like to layer, increase the size.

■ SIZE

38 (40, 42, 46, 50)" (96.5 [101.5, 106.5, 117, 127] cm) bust/ chest circumference. 33 (33, 34½, 34½, 36)" (84 [84, 87.5, 87.5, 91.5] cm) finished length. Sweater shown measures 42" (106.5 cm).

■ YARN

Super chunky-weight yarn, about 600 (660, 660, 720, 750) yd (549 [604, 604, 658, 686 m). We used Muench Yarns, GGH Fantastica (70% wool, 10% alpaca, 15% acrylic, 5% nylon; 30 yd [28 m]/50 g: 20 (22, 22, 24, 25) skeins, color #1, multi-colored blend of gold, rust, blue and red.

■ NEEDLES

Body and Sleeves—Size 15 (10 mm). Collar and Ribbing —Size 13 (9 mm). Adjust needle size if necessary to obtain the correct gauge.

■ NOTIONS

Tapestry needle; one covered hook and eye; safety pins.

■ GAUGE

7 stitches and 10 rows = 4" (10 cm) in stockinette stitch on size 15 (10 mm) needles.

■ STITCH GUIDE

1 × 1 rib (worked over a multiple of 2 stitches + 1)
Row 1: *Knit 1, purl 1*, end knit 1.
Row 2: Purl 1, *knit 1, purl 1*.
Repeat Rows 1 and 2 for pattern.

Stockinette Stitch
Row 1: (right side) Knit all stitches.
Row 2: Purl all stitches.
Repeat Rows 1 and 2 for pattern.

■ BACK

With larger needles, cast on 33 (35, 37, 41, 43) stitches. Work 1 × 1 rib until piece measures 8" (20.5 cm) from beginning, ending with a wrong-side row. Change to stockinette stitch and work even until piece measures 25 (25, 26, 26, 27)" (63.5 [63.5, 66, 66, 68.5] cm) from cast-on edge, ending with a wrong-side row. *Shape armholes:* Bind off 2 stitches at beginning of next 2 rows, then decrease 1 stitch each edge on next row and every other row 2 (2, 3, 3, 4) more times, working decreases on right-side rows as follows: knit 1, knit 2 together through back loop (see page 23), knit to last 3 stitches, knit 2 together, knit 1. Work even on 23 (25, 25, 29, 29) stitches until armhole measures 7½ (7½, 8, 8, 8½)" (19 [19, 20.5, 20.5, 21.5] cm) ending with a wrong-side row. *Shape neck and shoulders:* (right side) Bind off 3 (3, 3, 4, 4) stitches at beginning of next row—(one stitch on right hand needle). Knit across 2 (3, 3, 4, 5) stitches, join new yarn (see page 47) and bind off center 11 stitches, knit 5 (6, 6, 8, 9) stitches to end of row. Working each side of neck with a separate ball of yarn, bind off 3 (3, 3, 4, 4) stitches at beginning of next row and *at the same time* at each side of neck edge, bind off 1 stitch each side. Bind off remaining 2 (3, 3, 4, 4) stitches at each shoulder edge.

■ POCKETS

With larger needles, cast on 12 stitches. Work 5" (12.5 cm) in stockinette stitch. Change to 1 × 1 rib and work even for 2" (5 cm). Bind off all stitches loosely. Make one more pocket to match.

■ LEFT FRONT

With larger needles, cast on 17 (18, 19, 21, 22) stitches. Work 1 × 1 rib until piece measures 8" (20.5 cm) from beginning, ending with a wrong-side row. Change to stockinette stitch and work even until piece measures 25 (25, 26, 26, 27)" (63.5 [63.5, 66, 66, 68.5] cm) from cast-on edge, ending with a wrong-side row. *Shape armhole:* (right side) Bind off 2 stitches at beginning of next row. Purl 1 row. Decrease 1 stitch at beginning of next row and every other row 2 (2, 3, 3, 4) more times, working decreases on right-side rows as follows: knit 1, knit 2 together through back loop. Work even on 12 (13, 13, 15, 15) stitches until armhole measures 5" (12.5 cm), ending with a right-side row. *Shape neck:* With wrong side facing, bind off 4 stitches at beginning of row. Decrease 1 stitch at neck edge on next row and every other row 2 more times, working decreases as follows: knit to last 3 stitches, knit 2 together, knit 1. When armhole measures 7½ (7½, 8, 8, 8½)" (19 [19, 20.5, 20.5, 21.5] cm) bind off at shoulder edge 3 (3, 3, 4, 4) stitches once, purl 1 row, then bind off 2 (3, 3, 4, 4) stitches once.

■ RIGHT FRONT

Work same as for left front, reversing all shaping by binding off for armhole at beginning of a wrong-side row, and working neck shaping at beginning of a right-side row.

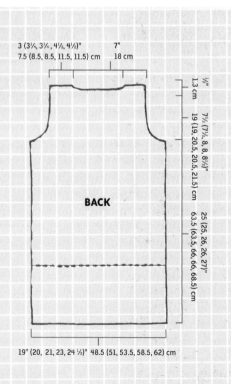

3 (3¼, 3¼ , 4½, 4½)"
7.5 (8.5, 8.5, 11.5, 11.5) cm

7"
18 cm

½"
1.3 cm

7½ (7½, 8, 8, 8½)"
19 (19, 20.5, 20.5, 21.5) cm

BACK

25 (25, 26, 26, 27)"
63.5 (63.5, 66, 66, 68.5) cm

19" (20, 21, 23, 24 ½)" 48.5 (51, 53.5, 58.5, 62) cm

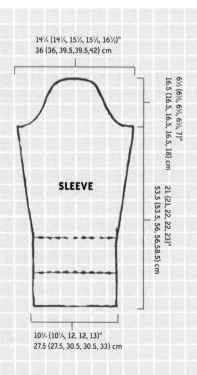

14¼ (14¼, 15½, 15½, 16½)"
36 (36, 39.5, 39.5, 42) cm

6½ (6½, 6½, 6½, 7"
16.5 (16.5, 16.5, 16.5, 18) cm

SLEEVE

21 (21, 22, 22, 23)"
53.5 (53.5, 56, 56, 58.5) cm

10¾ (10¾, 12, 12, 13)"
27.5 (27.5, 30.5, 30.5, 33) cm

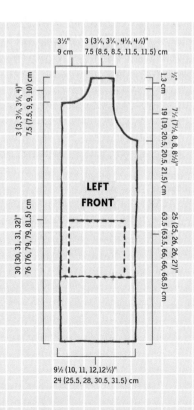

3½"
9 cm

3 (3¼, 3¼ , 4½, 4½)"
7.5 (8.5, 8.5, 11.5, 11.5) cm

½"
1.3 cm

3 (3, 3½, 3½, 4)"
7.5 (7.5, 9, 9, 10) cm

7½ (7½, 8, 8, 8½)"
19 (19, 20.5, 20.5, 21.5) cm

LEFT FRONT

30 (30, 31, 31, 32)"
76 (76, 79, 79, 81.5) cm

25 (25, 26, 26, 27)"
63.5 (63.5, 66, 66, 68.5) cm

9½ (10, 11, 12,12½)"
24 (25.5, 28, 30.5, 31.5) cm

SLEEVES

With larger needles, cast on 19 (19, 21, 21, 23) stitches. Work 1 × 1 rib until piece measures 8" (20.5 cm) from beginning, ending with wrong-side row. Change to stockinette stitch increasing 1 stitch each edge every 9 rows once, then every 10 rows 2 times—25 (25, 27, 27, 29) stitches— ending with a wrong-side row and piece measures 21 (21, 22, 22, 23)" (53.5 [53.5, 56, 56, 58.5] cm) from beginning. *Shape cap:* Bind off 2 stitches at beginning of next 2 rows. Decrease 1 stitch each edge every other row 6 (6, 6, 6, 7) times working decreases on second stitch from edge as for back and fronts—9 (9, 11, 11, 11) stitches remain. Bind off 3 stitches at beginning of next 2 rows. Bind off remaining 3 (3, 5, 5, 5) stitches. Make another sleeve to match.

COLLAR

With smaller needles, cast on 35 (35, 37, 37, 39) stitches. Work in 1 × 1 rib for a total length of 8" (20.5 cm). Bind off all stitches loosely.

FINISHING:

Block pieces to measurements. With yarn threaded on a tapestry needle and right sides of back and fronts together, sew shoulder seams using a backstitch (see Basics, page 92). Sew side seams using mattress stitch (see Basics, page 92). Pin pockets to fronts placing bottom edge of pocket along top of ribbing and side edge 1"(2.5 cm) from center front. Slipstitch invisibly (see Basics, page 93) in place. *Front Bands:* With smaller needles and right-side facing, pick up 56 (56, 58, 58, 60) stitches evenly along front edge (see page 47). Stitch pick-up ratio is about 2 sts for every 3 rows, although this may vary with individual knitters. Work 1 × 1 rib for 1½" (3.8 cm). Bind off all stitches. *Setting in Sleeves:* Sew sleeve seams using mattress stitch and reversing seaming 4" (10 cm) from bottom edge for turned back cuff. With right sides together, pin sleeves into armholes matching side seams and matching center top of sleeve to shoulder seam and easing remainder of sleeves to fit. Sew sleeve into armhole using backstitch. Using safety pins, pin cast-on edge of collar to neck edge, butting edges together and matching edges of collar to front edges of sweater and center of collar to center back of sweater. *Note: This will require quite a bit of easing of the neck edge to fit the collar edge.* With right side of work facing, slipstitch (see Basics, page 93) in place. Check inside edge of seam when you are done. In order to make the seam look good from both sides you may want to slipstitch on this side as well. Sew hook and eye on underside of front band at neck edge, aligning edges of hook and eye with edges of front bands. Weave in loose ends.

87

row counters

tape measure

point protecters

BASICS

Here's what you need to get started.

stitch holders

T-pins

■ **READING A PATTERN**

Most knitting projects are presented with written instructions called patterns. The pattern gives various sizes for the projects, the yarn, needles, and notions you'll need, the all-critical gauge (see page 90), and the particular stitch patterns that are used.

Instructions are given for each piece of a project. They begin with the number of stitches to cast on and they end with binding off those stitches. To save space, most instructions use standard abbreviations; however, the instructions in this book are written without abbreviations. For novice knitters, it's not always easy to know what the abbreviations in a pattern mean. First, get comfortable with your knitting, then knit projects that use the "knitter's shorthand."

Before you begin to knit, read through the instructions and make sure you understand how to do each part. Then read one sentence at a time. Each sentence represents one row of knitting or a series of rows that are worked the same way. Pay close attention to commas and semicolons because they usually indicate that something is changing in the next stitch or section. In some instructions, a series of stitches is repeated. The part to be repeated (called the pattern repeat) is usually set off with an asterisk (*) at either end.

double-pointed needles

tapestry needle

safety pins

Here are some common phrases in knitting patterns that will help you understand what to do.

Pattern Repeat

A pattern repeat refers to the number of stitches and rows that form a design in a unit. Different sizes of the same pattern will have a different number of pattern repeats across a row. A pattern repeat can contain as few as two stitches or as many as the width of the garment. When you're working a complex pattern, it is advisable to use stitch markers between repeats for easy counting and organization.

Pattern stitches will often be referred to as a "multiple of 4 + 2" or a similar combination. This term means that the total number of stitches is an even multiple of the first number, in this case 4, plus a single addition of the second number, in this case 2. The plus 2 balances a pattern within a garment so that a piece starts and ends with the same part of the pattern. For example, a 2 × 2 rib is a multiple of 4 stitches. If a 2 × 2 ribbing is to look balanced, two more stitches have to be added at the end so that each edge appears as a knit 2 on the right side of work.

Asterisk*

An asterisk is generally used to designate either end of a pattern repeat. It is a symbol used for bracketing so that whatever appears between the asterisks is repeated a designated number of times. For example, a pattern instructs "Knit 1, * knit 3, purl 5, knit 3, purl 2*. Repeat from * to * 3 times. Knit 1." This row is worked over 41 stitches. The beginning and ending "knit 1" are worked only one time each, while the instructions between the asterisks are worked three times.

Working Stitches as They Appear

As work faces you, knit or purl according to what you see. Unless the instructions specify otherwise, if you see a "V" under the loop you are about to work, knit the stitch, and if you see a "bump" under the loop, purl it. Generally, if you're working on rows and not in rounds, you work the opposite of what you worked on the previous row because the piece has been turned so that the opposite side is now facing you. If you're working in rounds, you repeat what you did on the previous round.

Marking Edges

Often a pattern directs you to mark an edge or edge stitch. This is usually in preparation for later work, such as where to begin sewing, or pick up stitches, or place a sleeve on a dropped shoulder. This marker will be removed later, but needs to be secure temporarily. Markers can be scraps of contrasting yarn tied to the stitch, safety pins, or split coil markers that can be slipped through the stitch.

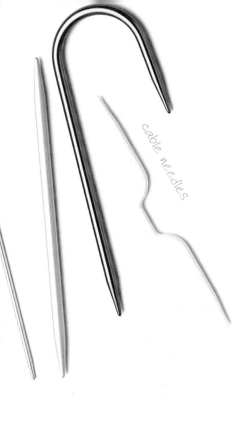

cable needles

Work in Pattern as Established

In a piece of knitting where the stitch count and pattern stitch remain the same, the repetition is automatic as the pattern stitch falls into line. When you're increasing or decreasing in a pattern stitch, you must make accommodations to incorporate more or fewer stitches. A common example is a sleeve that increases after the cuff. If it is difficult to isolate a pattern repeat, use stitch markers to designate complete pattern repeats.

In complex pattern stitches, increased stitches are worked in stockinette stitch until enough stitches are added to complete a full repeat, beginning the pattern stitch after the marker. In a simple pattern repeat, increased stitches can immediately be worked in pattern, but remember that stitches at the right-hand edge must be a mirror image of the left-hand edge. So in effect, you are adding stitches from the end of the pattern repeat and from the beginning.

Counting Rows

In stockinette stitch, each stitch appears as a V on the right side of the work and as a horizontal bump on the wrong side of the work. Look at either side of the work and at the vertical rows, and you'll see that this V or bump represents a row. Use a ruler and measure rows per inch or centimeter. It is most accurate to measure 4" (10 cm) of knitting and divide accordingly, especially when you're knitting with a thick and thin yarn. In cases where rows are difficult to distinguish, such as very dark colors or very long fibers like mohair, the best way to count rows is to work a swatch of the designated yarn, count the number of rows when you're knitting, and measure the entire swatch.

Right Side vs Wrong Side of the Ribbing

Look at the bottom edge of your cast-on stitches. There are two definite sides to a cast-on. What is usually considered the back or wrong side of the work bears most resemblance to a purl stitch. What is usually considered the right side of the work has a less distinguishable edge and looks like a slanted strand of yarn wrapped around the stitch—or at this point, a loop—on the needle. Since a balanced rib is half knit and half purl, the side to designate as "right side of work" really is a matter of preference, but conventionally the slant side is considered the right side.

■ KNITTING GAUGE

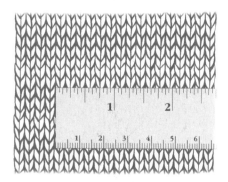

To check gauge, cast on 30 to 40 stitches using the recommended needle size. Work in the pattern stitch until the piece measures at least 4" (10 cm) from the cast-on edge. Remove the swatch from the needles or bind off loosely, and lay the swatch on a flat, hard surface. Place a ruler over the swatch and count the number of stitches across and number of rows down (including fractions of stitches and rows) in 4" (10 cm). Repeat two or three times on different areas of the swatch to confirm the measurements. If you have more stitches and rows than called for in the instructions, use larger needles; if you have fewer, use smaller needles. Repeat until gauge is correct.

Continental (long-tail) cast-on

Leaving a long tail (about ½" to 1" [1.3 to 2.5 cm] for each stitch to be cast on, plus a few extra inches to weave in later or use for seaming), make a slip-knot and place on right needle. Place the thumb and index finger of your left hand between the yarn ends so that the working yarn is around your index finger and the tail end is around your thumb.

Secure the ends with your other fingers and hold your palm upward to make a V of yarn (Figure 1).

Bring the needle up through the loop on your thumb (Figure 2).

Grab the first strand around your index finger with the needle and go back down through the loop on your thumb (Figure 3).

Drop the loop off your thumb and, placing your thumb back in the V configuration, tighten the resulting stitch on the needle (Figure 4).

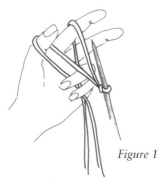

Figure 1

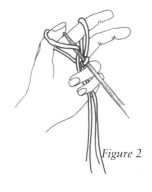

Figure 2

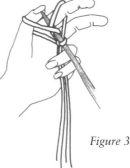

Figure 3

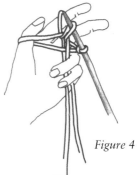

Figure 4

Basic Bind-Off

Slip 1 stitch, *knit 1 stitch, insert the left needle tip into the first stitch on the right needle.

Pass this stitch over the second stitch and slide off the needle*.

One stitch remains on the right needle and 1 stitch has been bound off. Repeat from * to * for the number of stitches to be bound off.

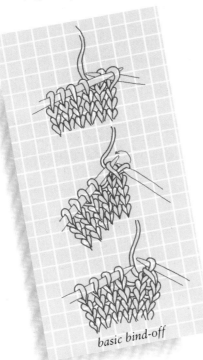

basic bind-off

Simple Increase—Knit into the Front and Back of a Stitch

Knit into a stitch but leave it on the left needle.

Knit through the back loop of the same stitch.

Slide the stitch off the left-hand needle.

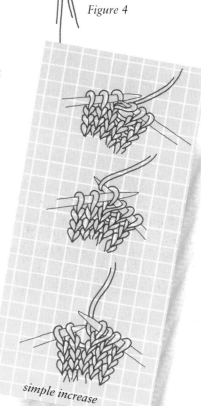

simple increase

91

Simple Decrease—Knit Two Together

Insert the right needle from front to back into the first two stitches on the left needle, working into the second stitch first, then the first stitch.

Knit both stitches together as if they were one. The stitches slant slightly to the right.

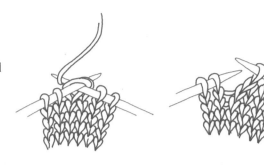

Slip a stitch

Insert the right needle into the stitch on the left needle as if you were going to purl it, but instead just slide the stitch onto the right needle. Here's a rule of thumb to remember when you're slipping stitches: Slip a stitch purlwise to avoid twisting it. Slip a stitch knitwise when it's part of a decrease or the instructions specify to do so.

slip a stitch

■ FINISHING STITCHES AND TECHNIQUES

Backstitch

This stitch is very firm and nonstretchy and it's usually used to sew shoulder seams together.

With the right side of the fabric facing you, pin together the two pieces to be seamed so that the edges are even. Working from right to left, one stitch in from the edge, bring a threaded tapestry needle under both Vs at the top of the bind-off edge and back through the first edge stitch. *Bring the needle through both fabrics again but move two stitches to the left and one stitch back.* Repeat from*, working back one stitch for every two stitches forward.

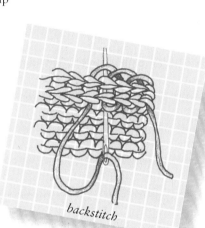

backstitch

Mattress Stitch on Stockinette Stitch

Working from the right side of the garment, place the pieces to be seamed on a flat surface, right sides up. Begin at the lower edge and work upward, row by row. Insert a threaded tapestry needle under two horizontal bars between the first and second stitches in from the edge on one side of the seam, and then under two corresponding bars on the opposite side.

Continue alternating from side to side, pulling the yarn in the direction of the seam, not outward toward your body, to prevent the bars from stretching to the front. When the seam is complete, weave the tail end down through the seam for two inches (5 cm).

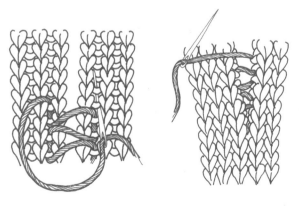

Mattress Stitch on Garter Stitch

Working from the right side of the garment, place the pieces to be seamed on a flat surface, right sides up. Begin at the lower edge and work upward, row by row.

Using a threaded tapestry needle, pick up the lower purl bar between the last two stitches on one piece, then the upper purl bar from the stitch next to the edge stitch on the same row of the other piece.

Continue alternating from side to side, pulling the yarn in the direction of the seam, not outward toward your body, to prevent the bars from stretching to the front. When the seam is complete, weave the tail end down through the seam for two inches (5 cm).

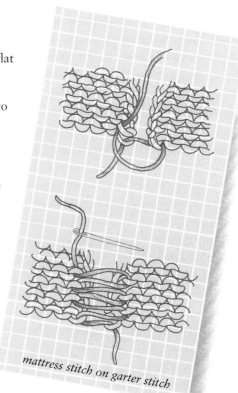

mattress stitch on garter stitch

Slipstitch (whipstitch)

Use this stitch or a variation thereof, to join two pieces of knitting together. You can join a finished edge to a piece of knitting or two edges together. This seam can be worked on either side of fabric depending on what pieces are being joined.

Blocking

There's one more step that adds that finishing touch to a knitted piece—blocking. This process helps eliminate any unevenness from your knitting, smooths the seams, and sets the drape. There are two ways of blocking, either by steam or wetting down the piece. It's preferable to block individual pieces before sewing them together as it can make the sewing process easier. But you can also block the whole piece once your project is sewn together.

You'll need a few things to block your garment—a surface you can stick pins into, rust-proof pins, a measuring device, and the finished dimensions of the piece. The surface can be as simple as a large towel spread out on a padded carpet or the top of your bed. The easiest pins to use are T-pins or pins with glass heads. The measuring device can be a yardstick or a nonstretching tape measure. Use the pattern schematic to check the size you're pinning your garment out to.

You can use your steam iron for steam blocking. Hold it a short distance above the hand-knit to allow the steam to penetrate the fibers. Once you've steamed the full surface, let it dry before removing the pins.

Wet blocking uses more moisture than steam-blocking and can be used to stretch and enlarge a knitted piece. Once you've pinned out the piece, use a spray-mist bottle with a fine, even mist. Gently pat the moisture into the handknit. Again, let it dry before you remove the pins. During the blocking process, steam or wet, remember not to flatten any raised stitches such as ribbing, bobbles, or cables.

YARN SUPPLIERS

Generic yarn weights and approximate yardages are provided in the patterns so you can easily substitute any weight yarn you want. Contact the companies listed below if you don't know of a local retailer or mail-order source for the yarns used in this book.

Baabajoes Wool Company
PO Box 260604
Lakewood, CO 80215
(303) 239-6313
www.baabajoeswool.com
Felted Tote Bag

Berroco, Inc.
14 Elmdale Rd.
Uxbridge, MA 01569
(508) 278-2527
www.berroco.com
Bare Necessities Purse

Brown Sheep Co., Inc.
100662 County Road 16
Mitchell, NE 69357
(308) 635-2198
www.brownsheep.com
Inner Child Mittens

Classic Elite Yarns
300 Jackson St.
Lowell, MA 01852
(978) 453-2857
Fluffy Muffler,
Fat Hats,
No Sleeves Funnel Top,
Boyfriend Sweater

Filatura di Crosa
8000 Cooper Ave.
Glendale, NY 11385
(718) 326-4433
www.tahkistacycharles.com
Tricolored Stocking Cap,
Mismatched Striped Socks

Garnstudio Yarns
U.S. Distributor: Aurora Yarns
PO Box 3068
Moss Beach, CA 94038-3068
(650) 728-2730
www.garnstudio.com
Everybody's Vest

GGH
U.S. Distributor: Muench Yarns
285 Bel Marin Keys Ste. J
Novato, CA 94949-5763
(415) 883-6375
www.muenchyarns.com
Stepping Out Coat

K1C2
2220 Eastman Ave. #105
Ventura, CA 93003-7794
(805) 676-1176
Dreamy Turtleneck

Manos Del Uruguay
U.S. Distributor: Design Source
38 Montvale Ave. Ste. 145
Stoneham, MA 02180
(888) 566-9970
A Must-Have Cardigan

Mission Falls
U.S. Distributor:
Unique Kolours
1428 Oak Ln.
Downingtown, PA 19335
(610) 280-7720
www.uniquekolours.com
No Sleeves Funnel Top

Morehouse Farm Sheep's Clothing
2 Rock City Rd.
Mileland, NY 12571
(845) 758-3710
www.morehousemerino.com
Hoodie Sweatshirt

Noro
U.S. Distributor: Knitting Fever
35 Debevoise Ave.
Roosevelt, NY 11575
(516) 546-3600
www.knittingfever.com
Seed Stitch Scarf

Rowan Yarns
U.S. Distributor: Westminster Fibers
5 Northern Blvd. #3
Amherst, NH 03031
(603) 886-5041
www.knitrowan.com
Most Basic Hat,
Mismatched Striped Socks

Tahki/Stacy Charles
8000 Cooper Ave.
Glendale, NY 11385
(718) 326-4433
www.tahkistacycharles.com
Fat Hats, Mismatched Striped Socks,
Rollover Pullover

Trendsetter Yarns
16742 Stagg St. #104
Van Nuys, CA 91406
(818) 780-5497
Ribbed Ribbon Tank Top

INDEX

FREE PATTERNS FROM EUROPE'S HOTTEST KNITTING MAGAZINE

INTERWEAVE
KNITS
FALL 2002

FALL'S BEST QUICK SWEATERS

Do *you* knit *in your* dreams?

Let *Interweave Knits®* make your dreams come true with—

- Knitwear designs to captivate your creative spirit
- Super-simple to challenging, traditional to cutting-edge styles
- A full range of sizing with you in mind
- Designer profiles, knitting stories from around the world, in-depth technical articles, the unexpected in every issue
- The latest news of yarns, tools, books, people, places, events

Essential Tools *for Every* Knitter!

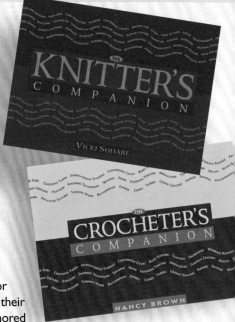

The Knitter's Companion
Vicki Square

If you have completed a sweater only to find that the buttonholes gape, ribbings flare, or seams pucker, or if you want to learn a variety of ways to cast on, shape, or seam a garment, this book is for you. It offers clear illustrated directions for dozens of knitting techniques including cast ons, bind offs, increases, decreases, joining yarns, buttonholes, seams, hems, and correcting mistakes, as well as tables of body measurements, yarn requirements, formulas, conversions and more—everything you'll need to know to size, knit, and finish a garment.
$19.95, Spiral-bound, 112 pages, ISBN: 1-883010-13-6

The Crocheter's Companion
Nancy Brown

This pocket-sized, spiral-bound reference for crochet-lovers is designed to fit into a project bag or basket, lie flat for easy use, and provide the essential information that crocheters need to have at their fingertips. From basic and advanced stitches, finishing techniques, and special touches, to time-honored favorite patterns, motifs, and medallions, this is an indispensable resource for serious and beginner crocheters alike.
$19.95, Spiral-bound, 112 pages, ISBN: 1-931499-13-6